The
Unwritten Curriculum

The Unwritten Curriculum

Things Learned But Not Taught in School

Arthur
Blumberg
Phyllis
Blumberg

CORWIN PRESS, INC.
A Sage Publications Company
Thousand Oaks, California

Copyright ©1994 by Corwin Press, Inc.

For information address:

 Corwin Press, Inc.
A Sage Publications Company
2455 Teller Road
Thousand Oaks, California 91320

SAGE Publications Ltd.
6 Bonhill Street
London EC2A 4PU
United Kingdom

SAGE Publications India Pvt. Ltd.
M-32 Market
Greater Kailash I
New Delhi 110 048 India

Printed in the United States of America

Library of Congress Cataloging-in-Publication Data

Blumberg, Arthur.
     The unwritten curriculum : things learned but not taught in school /
Arthur Blumberg, Phyllis Blumberg.
         p. cm.
     Includes bibliographical references (p. 120).
     ISBN 0-8039-6167-7 (cloth: alk. paper). — ISBN 0-8039-6164-2
(pbk. : alk. paper)
         1. School environment—Psychological aspects—Anecdotes.
     2. Interpersonal relations—Anecdotes. 3. School management and
     organization—Anecdotes. I. Blumberg, Phyllis. II. Title.
     LC210.B58   1994
     370.15'23—dc20   94–387

94 95 96 97 98   10 9 8 7 6 5 4 3 2 1

Corwin Press Production Editor: S. Marlene Head

Contents

Preface

Two ideas form the basis of this book. The first is that there is an informal and unplanned curriculum that is part of the daily life of youngsters in school. It is a curriculum whose content primarily stems from several sources: from the needs of adults to nurture children, from the fact that adults occupy positions of authority and power over youngsters, and from the needs of children to learn about learning and about relating to other youngsters and adults besides those in their families. Part of this curriculum simply evolves as a function of the formal organization setting of the school and how it operates to induce learnings about the system. There are also "electives," as it were, in this curriculum: learning experiences that result from happenstance.

The second idea is that, although the unwritten curriculum is not *taught* in any accepted sense of the word, it is nonetheless *learned*. Its operation is almost a pure example of experiential learning. The setting and the interactions that evolve from the relationships that adults and youngsters have with each other provide the circumstances and experience from which students, young and old, learn.

We use the term *unwritten* in the book's title and not *hidden* (Cowell, 1972; King, 1976; Snyder, 1971) because we want to avoid any implication that anyone has deliberately hidden the learning experiences about which we write. To the contrary, these experiences simply exist as a byproduct of the workings of the educational system and the behavior of the adults and the youngsters who are part of it. Further, when educators wish to develop a course or an entire curriculum, they put their proposals on the curriculum outline in writing and thus rationalize their endeavor. There is nothing prethought, preoutlined, or preplanned about the unwritten curriculum. As we noted, it simply exists.

We wrote this book for the following reasons: First, we believe it adds information and methodology to a neglected area of academic inquiry—the systematic investigation of both the content and circumstances of informal learning that takes place in schools. Second, and in some ways more important, the content and structure of the book provide a base for practical learning, through reflection and conversation, for three important groups of educators or would-be ones.

In the case of would-be educators, the book will be a valuable supplementary resource for students in teacher education programs, particularly at the point that they engage in student teaching. Its concern with the unwritten curriculum, as it stems in part from the unintended consequences of the behavior of teachers, makes it, we believe, an especially potent learning source for students as they begin to assume responsibility for a classroom. The book can also serve a useful purpose in courses such as, "Introduction to Education" or "The American School." It provides a type of information that is rarely discussed.

The second group for which this book has value is a school faculty concerned with staff development. It can and will serve as a basis for concern and reflection as a faculty moves to examine the typically unexamined and undiscussed side of student life in the schools.

The third group is composed of practicing school administrators and administrators in training. The book can help them gain insight into a side of school life of which they may be somewhat aware, but on which they have been unable to put a conceptual handle.

What makes this book different from other books or studies concerned with informal and unplanned learning in our schools is that both its content and structure involve stories or narrative accounts that adults, old and young, gave as they reflected on the query "If you think of your experience when you were a kid in school, what is the most vivid memory that immediately flashes into your mind?" The responses they gave to this question resulted in the following structure of the contents of the book that, through most of its chapter titles, extends the metaphor of "Unwritten Curriculum."

The book is divided into three parts: Part I, the Introduction, is subtitled "Unforgettable Impressions of School Life." The two chapters of Part I introduce the reader to the idea that an examination of the vivid and enduring memories each of us has of our years in school constitutes a viable method of understanding at least a part of the impact that schools, teachers, administrators, and peers have on school-age youngsters. In chapter 1, "Most Vivid and Enduring Memories of School," the basic concept of the book is explained as well as is the methodology by which the book was constructed and written. Chapter 2, "Going to School for the First Time," takes the reader to the very first days of school, with their accompanying excitement and anxiety. The reader will note how some of the outlines of "The Unwritten Curriculum" are formed early on.

Part II is called "Courses in the Unwritten Curriculum." Its chapters, 3 through 11, extend the curriculum idea through the unstated use of the word *course* in their titles. Thus, serially, we have courses in "Feeling Special in a Crowd," "When Caring Fosters Learning," "Being Physically or Emotionally Abused," "Being Embarrassed," "Experiencing Injustice," "Peer Relationships: Powerful Social Highs and Lows," "Battling the 'System': Sometimes a Winner and Sometimes a Loser," " 'Getting Even' by Playing Tricks and Pranks," and "Learning About Learning and Other Valuable Lessons."

In Part III we offer our "Conclusions" and summarize "What All This Means for Educators." Chapter 12, "Being Aware and Learning to Nurture," sets out what we think is the essential message this book of vivid memories of school contains.

There are, of course, any number of ways that this book can be used in undergraduate teacher education programs or in the schools. These uses are premised on the notion that the unwritten

xii THE UNWRITTEN CURRICULUM

curriculum should be made open to examination through talking about it. First and globally, it can serve as a trigger for individuals or groups to reflect on and talk about their own experience in school, with the idea of relating it to their present or prospective practice. Second, each chapter, perhaps each narrative in the book, can and should lead to a series of "I didn't know what to do when . . ." or "What would you have done . . ." problems that focus on some of the open-ended questions of school life.

One final note about the way the book is presented. With the exception of three bibliographic references in the Preface and two in the first chapter, no others are used throughout the text. This was a deliberate decision based on our belief that what awaits the reader is "everyone's" experience. The contents of the book are facts of school life and are not in need of a typical long list of references to enhance its credibility.

We have found the process of putting this book together a delightful one, but also one that, at times, made us shudder. It is our hope that the reader will share our delight and even our shuddering—and will also use the various narratives to reflect on life in the schools: what it is, what it is not, and what it might be.

We want to acknowledge with thanks the many people who contributed their most vivid school memories to our collection. We especially want to thank Cindy Dewberry-Moore for her wizardry with the word processor and Olympia Lira, a bit of a word processor wizard herself, who helped us out when we most needed her assistance.

ARTHUR BLUMBERG
PHYLLIS BLUMBERG

About the Authors

Arthur Blumberg is Professor Emeritus of Education in the School of Education at Syracuse University. He received his Ed.D. from Columbia University in 1954 and served on the faculty of Springfield College and Temple University prior to coming to Syracuse in 1967. His research and publication focused on administrative role relations. Among his books are *Supervisors and Teachers: A Private Cold War*, *The Effective Principal* (with William Greenfield), *The School Superintendent: Living With Conflict* (with Phyllis Blumberg), and *School Administration as a Craft*. These days he spends a good bit of his time traveling with his wife Phyllis and writing short essays that might be entitled "The World According to Arthur."

Phyllis Blumberg is currently on leave from her faculty position in the College for Human Development at Syracuse University. After 20 years as a homemaker and mother, she reentered college as a junior in 1968 and received her B.S. in 1970 and her M.A. in 1972, after which she was appointed a member of the faculty of the program in Marriage and Family Therapy at Syracuse. She completed her Ed.D. in 1978 and subsequently served her college for a number of years as Associate Dean. She has been an Approved Supervisor of the American Association for Marriage and Family Therapy since 1977. The Blumbergs have three married children and are proud grandparents of eight.

To all our grandchildren
with the hope
that their memories of school
will be fond ones

I

Introduction: Unforgettable Impressions of School Life

In this section, chapter 1 introduces the idea of how one's memory of past events and the way one speaks or writes about those events helps to create a montage of the unwritten curriculum. Chapter 2 deals, through the vehicle of memory narratives, with some initial experiences of school and the way they provide an early indication of the content of the unwritten curriculum.

Most Vivid and Enduring Memories of School

A quick way for the reader to get a sense of what he or she will encounter while proceeding through this book is to read the responses we got when we asked two adults the question, "If you think of your experience when you were a kid in school, what is the most vivid memory that immediately flashes into your mind?" One replied as follows:

This was in the fourth grade. I moved from Fresno, California to Chico. In Fresno, we did not learn cursive writing in third grade. When I went into fourth grade, the first day in Mrs. Elkins's room, there on the board was all cursive writing. I was terrified and I felt certain that I would be called upon to tell her what it said. So I sat there just petrified the whole entire day. I don't recall how she became aware that I did not know how to read cursive writing, but she did. She was very helpful and it was a wonderful year. She helped me learn to read the cursive stuff and never put me in a position of feeling inferior.

I still have a vision of the board. My next image of that classroom is kind of always standing beside her desk because I think I got a lot of individual care as a result of my terror.

The second person, with a chuckle, said,

I'm now 54. This happened at age 9. Mrs. English, my third-grade teacher, didn't like me and was always picking on me. One day, she was out part of the day and a substitute teacher took over. The substitute teacher made me the class monitor. I was standing in front of the room in that role when the substitute teacher went out and Mrs. English came back for the day, saw me in front of the room, took a ruler, and hit me with it. The next thing I remember happening was my mother came to school and said whatever mothers do to Mrs. English and the principal, and I wound up in a different third-grade class.

I was abused. Now I'm 54—that means that I have remembered this for 45 years. Mrs. English is now 136 years old and still beating the shit out of those kids.

In a nutshell, these two brief narratives are what this book is all about. It is a book of events that occurred in school that somehow imprinted themselves on the memories of people so that they were recalled, including the names of people involved, in some cases well over 50 years after the event took place.

Personal Stories as a Way to Make Sense of Experience

Storybooks, of course, are usually thought of in terms of children's reading. We believe, though, and for the following reasons, that the telling and reading of stories (not fiction) fill an important place in the learning and social life of adults.

Ultimately, we suppose, what life is about is each individual's effort to make sense of what has happened and what continues to happen to him or her. We do not think that, in most cases, these efforts take the form of deliberate analysis of life's events. Rather, it is our view that this sense-making process, for the most part, takes place as people work, raise families, take vacations, watch football games, go cross-country skiing—and then tell others about their experiences. The stories, in a way, describe our humanity. A case can be made for the idea that telling stories about life's experiences is integral to understanding what life is about. And the stories, of course, do not have to be, and probably are not, true in every detail. However, truth is not the issue here. What is the issue is that the stories we tell about our experience represent the lenses through which we wish to view that experience. (In the form of autobiography, they also present to the world, as Jerome Bruner [1987] suggested in a paper entitled "Life as Narrative," the image of us that we want others to hold.) In a way, they form the glue that holds the larger framework of our life together. At least, this is how *we* see things.

The "glue" idea was evident in an article by Elizabeth Stone (1988) that appeared in the *New York Times Magazine*. Entitled "Stories Make a Family," it is Stone's account of how stories about her Italian immigrant family passed from generation to generation, thus lending substance to them, and in the process creating a family saga that became a source of laughter, pride, and, we suspect, some tears. Mostly, though, it seems to be reasonable to think that family storytelling creates a shared sense of people becoming bonded to each other both in the present and also, as we noted, in an intergenerational sense.

We came across this intergenerational bonding or "gluing" idea as one function of storytelling in another context. It was Hanukkah, the Jewish Festival of Lights, and, of course, there is a story attached to it. A local newspaper ran a feature article about the holiday and quoted a rabbi who was visiting a Jewish play school as saying to the youngsters, "I have to tell you the story of Hanukkah." Note the use of "I have to." It was not a matter of "I want to" or "It would be nice to." No, it was a matter of compulsion—the essence of the tradition is carried on through stories.

Memories and Stories of School

Schools, however, are neither families nor religions; neither are they institutions for which people, except in rare cases, seem to have thought it necessary in any universal sense to create an intergenerational tradition through one vehicle or another. Why, then, a storybook about them? Or, to put it more squarely, Why a book made up of stories based on memories of experiences in school?

We have thought a good bit about that question, trying to answer another: What is it that a book of stories about school would have to offer besides a few chuckles and a pleasant nostalgic experience? Two answers emerged for us as we read and reread the narratives we collected. The first had to do with the idea that the collection and analysis of vivid memories that adults retain of their experience in school is a type of knowledge that is somehow important to develop and understand. In a little more detail, what we mean is described below.

It is true that the huge majority of the time of a school day is devoted to the formal activities of teaching and learning. However, it is also true that simply by going to school a youngster is guaranteed to have other experiences that are not part of the formal school curriculum but in many ways, although not measurable, are possibly of greater impact. Next to one's family, school is the institution in which most time is spent in a youngster's growing years. Nevertheless, school, different from the primary group culture of the family, is a secondary group, one in which the intimacy so valued by the family, for example, is not attended to in any systematic way. The point we want to reinforce, then, is that going to school typically represents a child's first venture into a world of organizational life. And in this life youngsters start to experience, for the first time outside the family group, and therefore differently, the gamut of events and the accompanying emotionality that will be part and parcel of their adult years.

Although children certainly come in contact with such matters as love, hate, closeness, distance, warmth, coolness, rewards, punishment, competition, cooperation, and freedom and control before they go to school, they do so within a group context that is, by definition, nurturing. When they step inside the schoolhouse door, they implicitly contract to experience these same conditions of life (and more) over a period of 12 or 13 years within a group context where nurturance is not a norm but where it might occur by chance.

These thoughts lead us back to our first answer to the question, What is it that a book of stories about adult memories of school might have to offer beyond a bit of humor and nostalgia? We think that it can offer a glimpse into a side of life that occurs in schools that is obtainable in no other way. That is, *in a sense, these stories and untold numbers of others like them constitute a type of knowledge about schools that needs to take its place alongside other bodies of school-related knowledge.*

Why should we write about stories that are almost certainly inaccurate in their detail, filtered as they are through the teller's memory? We think the answer is pretty straightforward. To tell a story is to engage in what is probably one of humankind's oldest modes of communication. To tell a story may well be as natural an action as is laughing and crying. So the body of this book may be a way of representing "what comes naturally." Even though the facts of the story may have become jumbled, we suspect that the image symbolized in the story is reliable.

The second answer to the question, Why such a book as this? is a more practical one. We think that school teachers, school administrators, and would-be ones (much as parents or college teachers) need to be reminded that, not infrequently, in one fashion or another *what they do and what happens to kids in school gets remembered.* Sometimes the memories are pleasant ones and sometimes they are unpleasant. This difference will become very apparent as the reader moves through the book.

Collecting and Organizing the Stories

We went about collecting the stories in two ways. First, in classes of both graduates and undergraduates, we simply asked our students to write about something that had happened while they were in school that stood out vividly in their minds as they thought back to the school experience. We asked our secretaries to do the same thing. A colleague of ours on the faculty of another college did us the favor of making a similar request of her students. Second, we collected stories via tape recorder from both students and professors who walked in our offices for whatever reason. We also were told stories by friends and acquaintances in a variety of other places, including the porch of our rented summer cottage on Cape Cod.

Obviously, our respondents were both male and female. Most were Caucasian but there were also some African-American and Hispanic respondents. Although we did not keep a close tally of this, most of our respondents came from a middle- or lower-middle-class background. A few came from lower socio-economic brackets. The age range was from 18 to 74, the eldest being an African-American woman in the process of earning an undergraduate degree. All told, we collected 220 stories.

Our next step was to organize the stories into categories. We did this by reading each story and making a decision about its essential focus. It was not an easy thing to do. For example, sometimes the stories were centrally concerned with an individual, sometimes with an event, and sometimes with both. There were also some stories that were unrelated to the school as a purposeful institution but were related to the fact that the school simply provided the setting for something to happen that would not have happened if there had been no school. There were also a number we discarded as inappropriate for what we wanted to accomplish.

As an aside, we should note that the very act of reading the stories was an educational experience in itself. We laughed at the pranks that were recalled and at the funny things that stayed in people's minds; we were shaken by the memories of events that were far from funny. There were, indeed, memories of being abused. We were touched by the nurturance that was associated with the memory of a student-teacher relationship, we were struck by the vividness of the image that was held of an outstanding teacher, and we were impressed by the cruelty that youngsters can exhibit toward each other.

What emerged from our analysis and organization of the content of the anecdotes was the structure of the bulk of the book: its contents.

We have little doubt that others might well come up with different categories. Some colleagues, for example, have suggested that we focus on matters of authority—little people, big people. Others have thought that a way to do the job was to put it into a developmental perspective, that is, to think in terms of growth patterns of youngsters. Although not always immediately agreeing with each other, we chose to separate things in a way that we thought would help most readers recall their own school life and relate it to the idea of the unwritten curriculum. We were interested in putting together a book to which people could relate intellectually, emotionally, and practically, not in the development of a theoretical or scientific treatise. And so we have what we have. We also need to take note of the fact, as the reader will most certainly discover, that the contents of all the categories are not scientifically discrete. Nor could they be. People, events, and emotions are too entwined to make for the kind of surgical separation that may be desirable in some settings—but not here.

There are a few other caveats that must be attended to in this introductory chapter. First is the matter of the sample of people who provided us with their memories of school. It is obvious, as we indicated above, that it was by no means a random sample nor did we make an effort to randomize it. We simply were not interested in being "scientific" but only in opening up the world of the school to be thought of and talked about in a different way. Even though we did not engage in efforts to develop a representative sample, we have every confidence that, for most intents and purposes, we have covered the range of categories of memories that people have about their school experience. We are pretty sure that practically every reader will have a recollection of a school or school-related event that will fit someplace in our unwritten curriculum scheme.

There is an additional and elaborative point about the people who recalled their "most vivid" school experience for us. As noted, they are all people who either were currently in college or graduate school, or they are older adults who had been to college or graduate school. Thus we leave out a large segment of the population in our sample. However, we are convinced, and we have tested this informally, that their memories, too, would fall into the categories we already have.

Second, although most of the anecdotes come from public school experience, a number are from Catholic schools, and some are from other types of private schools. The reader will find that a number of the Catholic school-related memories are negative ones, although some are mixed. In no way do we propose that the memories of Catholic school experience that were recalled for us are representative of what those schools were like, any more than might be the case with the public schools. They are, however, representative of the memories that people called up when asked.

The third caveat has to do with the matter of interpretation of the data. Our objective is to present each category of memories of the unwritten curriculum without becoming overly interpretive about it and to *let the storytellers speak for themselves.* What they have to say is much more important than our commentary might be. In this connection, the reader will find that we make no use of references throughout the elaboration by story of the unwritten curriculum. Nor do we apologize for this.

Several other thoughts are noteworthy in this introduction. First, it will be seen that in most cases where a teacher is the focal point of the memory, the name of the teacher (which we have changed as well as names of places) is recalled along with the event. This thought attracts us not because we consider it strange but because it reminds us of the potentially powerful impact that a teacher may have on a youngster. Some of the memories we report, as we noted previously, go back well over 50 years. In an informal but related study we conducted, an interview with a 97-year-old woman revealed her memory of the names of her teachers in Grades 1 through 4.

Second, we need to say that although we include memories of what were undoubtedly traumatic experiences, as might be expected, they are looked back on today with smiles, if not laughter. We certainly do not condone the occurrence of these experiences, and it may well be that some youngsters have their perspectives on school affected by them for a long period of time. Somehow, though, most of us manage to live with them and even to laugh at them.

In this connection, it is interesting to note that the category that contained the most memories (before some were discarded to achieve a better balance) had to do with being embarrassed. The reader may make of that whatever he or she wishes. The only general comment we can offer is to say that, when asked, many of our respondents seemed quite prone to remember a negative school experience rather than a positive one.

The reader will recall that some of the memories we collected were in writing and some were obtained via tape recording. This difference will show up occasionally in the way the story reads. Some are crafted better than others but we hope that with the aid of a little judicious editing, they are all readable.

Another point has to do with the varying strength of the emotional content of the stories. Some of them are very powerful, whereas some seem almost bland. With regard to the latter, we think it is worth noting that through our analytical and dispassionate eyes it is a bit hard to understand why bland experiences should be remembered. The only thing we can say is that for the person involved it apparently was not a bland experience at all.

Finally, there are two structural comments that need to be made. The first is that although chapter 2, "Going to School for the First Time," logically starts things out, there is no thematic connection between or among the following chapters. Each may be read without regard to what preceded it or what follows it. There is no progession of thought from chapter to chapter, although taken together, of course, they do make for a larger picture.

Second, in similar fashion to this point about the chapter-by-chapter structure, there is no thematic connection between or among the anecdotal memories presented in each chapter. Taken together, they also make for a larger picture.

And, as we pause to think about it, it is a *very* large picture, indeed.

Going to School for the First Time

"Just think, as soon as we come back from vacation you'll be going to kindergarten."

"Next year you'll be big enough to go to school just like your sister."

"I can hardly believe that you're big enough to go to school."

Comments such as these are repeated, we suspect, by the million every year as a new wave of 5-year-olds prepares to take the grand step from home to school. Parents, grandparents, aunts, uncles, and friends speak these words to a little girl or boy, and they tend to be music to the ear (or, at least, that is what adults think). No longer will he or she be a homebound child. Life for the youngster will start to take on wings, as it were. This is true not only for the kindergartner, as his or her going to school also signifies a change in parental lives.

In a way, it is probable that, at least in the youngster's imagination, school's first days occur long before he or she ever sets foot inside the schoolhouse. That is, the way we talk about going to school, about all the fun it will be, about how "you'll be able to read your books by yourself," about how "you'll have to mind your teacher"—these and many other thoughts like them create images of what school will be like. It will be work, it will be play, and it will make you independent. This

11

and much, much more. It is also likely that no other event in a youngster's first 5 years receives so much emphasis. It is certainly a period that separates two stages of life.

With such universal attention given to the start of going to school, it was a little surprising to us that adult memories of "going to school" did not contribute more heavily to our story collection. However, as we talked with each other, it developed that neither of us has any explicit memory of going to school on that first day, although we did dredge up memories of having been in kindergarten. Perhaps the reason for the relative lack of vivid recall of the first day of school is that the very newness, the large number (comparatively) of people gathered in one place, or the many different activities create a blur in our minds, making sharp memories of that day hard to come by. Nothing startling happens that gets imprinted in our minds for future recall, or so it seems for many of us.

There are a few stories, however, that fit in well with the notion of the unwritten curriculum. The rather matter-of-fact observation that a child may start to experience the unwritten curriculum on his or her first day at school—and even learn from it—was a bit startling. The fact seems to be that what is informal and unplanned starts to make its presence known, although most certainly not understood, early on in a child's very first venture into the school building. Thus we have a memory of being intimidated by authority in "Too Scared to Tell Her My Right Name," and other stories that involve abandonment and the conflict between "being on one's own" and the more secure and warm feeling of being nurtured within the family. In one way or another, issues of nurturance and power seem to recur throughout the school experience and, as we indicated, it is likely that it all begins on Day 1.

Too Scared to Tell Her My Right Name

When I started in kindergarten, my mother took me to school the first day. She said to the teacher, "My first name is Celia and the woman who is going to pick Leah up after school also has the first name of Celia." Well, my mother left and then the teacher called us by name to sit around in a circle. I figured out right away that what had happened was that the teacher had gotten my mother's story wrong because she called me Celia. I let her do that because I was too scared to say anything. My mother was working full-time so she didn't come to school for about 6 weeks. When she finally came to school, they were still calling me Celia. My mother kept referring to me as Leah. Finally, she realized that the teacher was not confused as to which kid she was talking about when she was talking about me, but she was calling me the wrong name and I was too intimidated to tell her.

He Left Me—I Cried

I was 4 years old when I went to kindergarten at Elwood school. My father took me there the first day and then he left me. I didn't know where he had gone. He went to the bathroom, which was right in the classroom, but I thought he left me for good and I cried and cried. I stood right at the door waiting for him to come out, even though they told me he was there. But I still cried and I cried for a whole week, or at least it seemed that way. We talked about it—my mother and I—for years after that and my mother used to say, "Remember that?" Particularly, I remembered when my own children went to school. I made sure they didn't have those problems—the same kind of problems that I did—at having felt left.

On My Own

I was looking forward to going to school. The school, like most public schools, was in my neighborhood. It was about two blocks away and kids walked, of course. Each day, my sister, who was 3 years older than me, would go to school and I would wait for her to come home. But I couldn't wait to join her in school and do the same as she had been doing. All of my life it was always my sister who would do it first and I would come next. Well, it came time for me to go to kindergarten and my mother walked me up the two blocks to the school. I was really excited about this and I got to the sidewalk and my mother said, "OK, go in through those doors and I'll see you— say in 2 hours—eleven o'clock." That was the first time I realized that I was going to do this on my own. And I just panicked. I said, "What do you mean?" And she said, "I'll see you in 2 hours. You go in there by yourself." I cried. She actually had to walk me through the doors and bring me to the teacher. However, I remember being too embarrassed to cry in the classroom, which is kind of interesting. So when the teacher took over I stopped crying. I cried from the moment my mother left me at that sidewalk to the moment I walked into the teacher's room. It was the first time I knew that I had to do it on my own.

I Couldn't Wait to Get There

I remember my kindergarten teacher. Her name was Miss Anton. I first met this teacher in June of 1954. I had received an invitation from her to visit her classroom one afternoon in June. I remember the excitement of, first, receiving my own piece of mail and, second, going to school for the first time.

I remember getting all dressed up and walking with my mother the three short blocks to the school. Then we walked into what seemed to be an amazingly large building, and I remember holding fast to my mother's hand. I thought that if we got separated I'd never find my way out. And I still remember how tightly I held my mother's hand when we walked into the classroom. I was scared and yet excited about the whole experience.

Miss Anton was waiting at the front door and greeted my mother and me very warmly.

I remember walking into the classroom in awe of all the things around me. I remember Miss Anton asking the class if anyone knew who I was. When Susan, the girl who lived across the street from me, said that she did, Miss Smith invited her to show me around the classroom. I was allowed to walk freely about and explore the variety of learning centers. Kindergarten looked like such fun I couldn't wait to get there.

They Had Bathrooms There, Just Like Home

Walking down the steep hill seemed like fun in the beginning. It wasn't until we were about halfway down that I felt the backs of my legs beginning to cramp a little from trying to hold back. My mother's hand was sweaty, and although she always spoke of school being in the fall, it seemed like a summer day to me: warm, sunny, and no jacket. I remember the skipping and swinging kind of game we played as we walked down that steep hill to the school. A tonsillectomy had prevented me from starting kindergarten with the rest of the kids. However, the 2 weeks' delay had only heightened my excitement and anticipation of this wonderful place called school my mother had so often told me about.

Finally, we came to the bottom of the hill and the busy street with the stoplight. "Now remember Allan, always wait for the green light, look both ways, and cross only when it's safe. Be sure to look for Mrs. Cotta the crossing guard. She will help you." After crossing the street, my mother talked with Mrs. Cotta for a moment. We passed six more houses, an open space, and there it was, very tall with lots of red bricks, brown steel doors, and fences on the windows. My mother told me the fences on the windows were there to keep the baseballs from breaking the glass during recess. I was most amazed and impressed with the bigness of everything and, although it was 1946 and I was only 5 years old, I can still remember the smells and sounds of that first day. I remember the smell of cleaning stuff, and paste, and finger paint, and Miss Limus, my kindergarten teacher. She smelled like my Aunt Mary, who would sometimes baby-sit for me. I also remember the room, the wood benches, and the black phone on the wall with no dial.

Miss Limus was very nice and welcomed me to the class. She explained to everyone that I had just been in the hospital and asked if I wanted to tell the class about my experience. It was not an occasion I wanted to remember, so I just shook my head, no. I remember that we all sat on the floor in front of Miss Limus and I noticed that she had the same kind of underwear my mother wore, the kind with funny metal clips attached to the tops of the stockings. It made me feel so comfortable.

The day was progressing wonderfully and I was really enjoying my belated first day at school. Then it happened, right in the middle of playing with blocks I started to get that familiar bubbly feeling in my lower stomach, and I knew I would soon need to visit the bathroom. I went to Miss Limus and discreetly whispered my need into her ear, and she said out loud, "Of course, Allan, you may go to the bathroom," and she motioned to the door across the room. I went out the door and found I was in the same corridor I had come down with my mother earlier. I walked down the hall past the little room with the sounds of clicking and ladies talking until I came to the big steel doors. I pushed hard on the shiny gold-colored bar across the door and squeezed out onto the street. I walked past the six houses to the busy street with the stoplight and looked for Mrs. Cotta, the crossing guard. She wasn't there. I waited until the light turned green, looked both ways, and crossed the street. As I climbed the big steep hill I remember thinking, the next time I have to go to the bathroom I will have to ask sooner, because climbing the hill made it too hard to hold in.

I remember the horrified look on my mother's face when she opened the door. At the time I couldn't imagine why she was so upset. After all, I was able to hold it, and I didn't dirty my pants. As I sat there on the toilet, I could hear her in the kitchen talking to someone on the phone. I heard long words that I could say but didn't know the meanings of. Words like responsibility and communication and I heard her talk about the busy street, and the most astounding thing of all, I was sure

I heard her say something about the bathrooms at school! When she got off the phone she came to see how I was doing. She asked if the teacher had shown me where the bathroom was at school. I was so amazed at the thought. Imagine that! They had bathrooms at school just like at home, and black phones, without dials, on the wall. What a wonderful place!

II

Courses in The Unwritten Curriculum

As we mentioned in the Preface, each chapter title in Part II begins with the unstated "A Course in . . ." That is, it is our assumption that each of the experiences related to us induced some type of learning in the narrator. Indeed, the reader will find that from time to time in the narratives the point is made in almost those very words. What will be found in these various "courses" are memories that have to do with nurturance, the abuse of power, learning about peer relations, the meaning of the "system," and learning itself.

Together, these several chapters constitute "The Unwritten Curriculum" as we understand it.

Feeling Special in a Crowd

This chapter focuses on memories of a teacher who dealt with a pupil in a way that communicated to the pupil that the teacher was concerned about his or her welfare, physical or emotional, simply as adult to child. Some of the memories seem to deal with rather inconsequential things. For example, one has to do with a teacher having provided, unsolicited, a Band-Aid for a pricked finger. We must admit we find the fact that some people vividly recall such little things to be a bit puzzling, because from our disinterested viewpoint they hardly constitute a memorable event. But then, our eyes and ears were not those of the beholders and receivers of these experiences. Also, some memories were reported to us that even a jaundiced-eyed adult would describe as rather profound.

Perhaps there is a lesson for all of us in these narratives. It is that one simply never knows what will be remembered—and this may be a call to be more aware of oneself and what one does or does not do as a teacher (and, we must add, as a parent).

We need to push this last point a bit further. We have observed the goings-on in many schools, in hallways as well as in classrooms. We have seen teachers and principals react to problems they encounter with students with compassion and concern as well as with distance and harshness. We have seen teachers correct and discipline children in such a manner that the youngster sensed adult concern with his or her welfare. We have observed the opposite, where it seemed as though the child was little more than an irritant to be scratched away. We have observed youngsters who were treated as if they were objects, with the teacher maintaining as much interpersonal distance from them as possible, or so it seemed. And we have seen adults treating youngsters in school with a softness that simply made us marvel.

Frankly, we do not understand how these differences come about. We believe that the great bulk of teachers start out in their work interested in youngsters, their learning, and their general welfare. In some cases, however, it seems something happens along the way. The work of teaching, its ultimate and honorable meaning, becomes transformed into a mere job, a means of making a living. We suspect that when this happens, the incidence of "just and caring" behavior on the part of the teacher wanes.

Few of the stories about feeling "special" or cared for have much of a dramatic flair about them. Perhaps it is true that, for the most part, pleasant memories are soft and gentle ones. This is a thought that is in need of some elaboration. We have noted previously that although there are indeed gentle and nurturing teachers and administrators in schools, schools themselves are not necessarily gentle and nurturing institutions. We suspect that the case is quite the opposite, although most of us would prefer it to be otherwise. Thus, in what follows, it may be that the soft and gentle experience of feeling cared for is variant enough from the cool detachment of the institution to create a memorable experience. The reader can test that hypothesis against his or her own experience.

In any case, an important message of this book—that adults remember how they were dealt with in school—starts with "My Birthday Was in July."

My Birthday Was in July

This is a story about when I was in kindergarten. I don't know, maybe it was because I was still struggling to learn English (we had come from Europe) that this was rather interesting. I went to a public school. I noticed that whenever there was a birthday they made a big to-do, and the kids would all sing "Happy Birthday!" to the child that had the birthday. It was a big thing. Well, I guess I wanted to be accepted, too, and I realized that my birthday was in July and nobody was ever going to sing "Happy Birthday!" to me. So, one day I went in and with a very straight face I told the teacher it was my birthday. She must have known it wasn't but she went along with it and she had all the kids sing "Happy Birthday!" to me. I don't remember the teacher's name, but I just thought that was awfully nice of the teacher to just gloss it over—just to kind of help me out. It made me feel part of things.

Exclusion and Inclusion

One incident that has always stayed on my mind happened in the fourth grade. A very studious girl named Sandy became the class scapegoat. Everyone called her names and excluded her from the class activities, except me. I never held anything against Sandy, because to me she was a nice girl and a good friend. It bothered me that people never got to know Sandy, because if they took the time to talk to her they would have met a loyal and down-to-earth person. What's funny is that these people were the ones that talked about each other behind their backs.

During parent conferences that year, my teacher, Mrs. Eckle, told my mother how I was the only child in the class who was nice to Sandy. They both thought that it was a praiseworthy thing to do. I did not think that I deserved any credit. It was simply the proper way to act. Besides, I would not want to be treated in that manner.

In sixth grade I got Mrs. Eckle as a teacher again. A few weeks after school started, she pulled me aside and told me that there was a girl named Lisa who wasn't really fitting in with the rest of the girls. She asked me if I would include Liz in my free-time activities. Well, I did and Liz became a good friend of mine. I don't think I will ever forget Mrs. Eckle, Sandy, or Lisa.

Just Three People

In junior high school I remember being in ninth grade, and I had a history teacher who was Mr. Smith. And I remember somehow that I was top dog in that class. During study hall, a friend and I convinced Mr. Smith to coach us as we hit tennis balls back and forth in the gym. This was totally taboo but we did it anyhow. That was very special because it was just the three of us having a get-together. You know, it had nothing to do with history or social studies or anything, and it was just a lot of fun. It was very human. Just three people together, two pupils and a teacher. That was more important than history.

A "Freedom-to-Feel" Pass

I had a really tough time in chemistry. I remember one day when I was not in a very good mood. I don't even remember why I was upset. I just remember that I was exceptionally out of sorts. Normally, when I walked in the room I would joke around. This day I didn't. I went right to my seat and sat down and didn't say a word to anybody that looked at me crosswise. About 5 or 10 minutes into the class, my teacher stopped lecturing and he said, "Excuse me for 1 minute." He went to his desk and he wrote something and he came to the front of the room and he said, "I really need to have this message brought to the office. It's something I forgot." And he said, "Jane, will you bring it down for me?" And I said, "Sure." I wanted to get out of there anyway. I was really upset. So I took it and I walked out. When I got out in the hall, he came out in the hall and he said, "Just a minute." Then he said, "This is a 'freedom-to-feel' pass. You can take as much of this period as you would like to go to the library. It is obvious that you are upset about something. Take the time to just sit quietly and get rid of what it is that is bothering you. Go to the library, go to the nurse's office, go to the counselor's office. I trust you to use this sensibly."

He was very sensitive to my feelings. And so I did just what he suggested. What I did was go in and talk with my guidance counselor whom I considered a friend at that point. I felt comfortable with him. And afterwards, I just thanked my teacher for doing what he did.

He Gave Me a Band-Aid

This memory I have is from third grade. My teacher's name was Mr. Johns and I was his favorite. One day he asked a few of us to help him put up a new bulletin board. He put me in charge of stapling all of the pieces of construction paper on the board. I had to use one of those staplers that you have to open up to use on the wall. I was holding one of the pieces of paper and was trying to staple it and I put the staple through my thumb. It didn't really hurt but I let out a little yell. Mr. Johns came over and just pulled it out and gave me a Band-Aid. It was good to feel cared for.

I Lost My Nickel

It was in second grade. This was during the depression and we used to bank a nickel or a dime one day a week. Once I lost my nickel and I was just devastated. That was a big deal! The teacher said, "Why don't you go look for it. I'll send Francis out with you." Francis was this older kid and he found the nickel. I thought, "Isn't this magnificent!" What would have turned out to be a disaster, losing my nickel, turned out OK. And it wasn't until years later when I thought, "How the hell did Francis ever find the nickel?" As I thought about it, the teacher had to have given the nickel to him. That must have been it, and she probably said to Francis, "Here's a nickel and pretend that you found it." It was a very good idea and nice thing. She was really human.

The Concrete Cake

It was a cold blustery day in February, when I woke up with butterflies in my stomach. I was in kindergarten, assigned to the morning section with Mrs. Williams. The reason for the excitement was that it was my sixth birthday! I took the bus into school, thinking about my birthday the whole way. I couldn't concentrate on singing "Puff the Magic Dragon." I kept waiting for "the special moment." Finally, Mrs. Williams gathered everyone around the side table and pulled out the cake! They all sang "Happy Birthday!" to me. I was thrilled! Then she put the concrete cake away for the next birthday.

We Would Never See Him Again

My sixth-grade teacher, Jack Larson, was the first male teacher I encountered in elementary school. And, oh, how I loved and respected him (as did everyone who was in our class)! He cared about us, he trusted us, and he respected us as human beings.

At the end of that school year, Mr. Larson told us he was leaving our district and moving to Philadelphia. That meant that not only were we leaving his class but we knew we would never see him again.

The last day of school was so difficult—saying good-bye, knowing we'd never talk to him again. My best friend, Susie, and I stayed at school all day (even though we were allowed to leave at 10:00). We hung out in his room while he packed and took care of all of his 'end-of-year' duties, just chatting with him, not wanting to let go. But, we finally left (in tears), saying our final farewell.

Then, 2 years later on a school evening, my phone rang. It was Jack Larson calling me from Philadelphia. He just wanted to say hello and see how I was doing. He remembered; he cared.

When Caring Fosters Learning

The memories that make up "When Caring Fosters Learning" seem to provide part of the answer to the question, What are the ingredients of a good teaching-learning situation? Chapter 4 is composed of memories of classroom situations concerning the development of a relationship between teacher and student that enabled the student to devote energy to learning, to overcome obstacles to learning, or, it is hoped, to enjoy learning. Included are examples where a teacher somehow communicated to a student that his or her learning was important, and the student was motivated to learn and felt valued and cared for as a person. If there is a sadness about chapter 4, it is that so few of the memories that were reported to us involved these circumstances.

This Guy Kept Me Alive

The first class I ever took from this teacher was sixth-grade English and sixth-grade mathematics. He was a good teacher and I remember feeling about him very favorably, because I learned my arithmetic and my multiplication tables from him. We had to study this until we could do it in a time test that we had to take. When we could go through this chart in the proper time, then we were released from that obligation. But the major thing that I remember in taking English from him was being able to take apart sentences and know all the figures of speech, so that when I went into the upper grades I really didn't have to study any more because I had already had it.

Anyway, the next time I encountered him was in 11th grade when I took plane geometry. I just couldn't get plane geometry. I mean I struggled with it and I couldn't get it, and that was a little bit surprising because I had done very well in algebra the year before. Mathematics came easy for me, but I couldn't figure out plane geometry. I just did terribly poorly on my monthly tests. I was getting 40s, but my report card would come home and I would have a D for the month, not an F. And of course, my test scores didn't jive with the report card. So, one day my mother went to see this teacher and asked him about this. She said, "Mister Rinson, why is this happening? I don't understand. He does not deserve his grades based on his test scores. I must admit that he has told us about them, and he's quite concerned about his problems that he's having with this. And he himself is wondering why he is getting these Ds." He said, "Well, the reason I'm giving him Ds is because I'm fully convinced that he'll catch on to this very soon and when he does, I'm sure his grades will come right on up." He said, "I don't want to start giving him grades now which would impact his getting into college."

Isn't that neat? So, by golly, in about the third or fourth month, suddenly the light came on and I really caught on to the logic of plane geometry. The net result of that was I got 100s in my midterm examination, so this guy kept me alive.

One Teacher Really Cared

There was my 11th-grade physics teacher, Father Raymond, who would spend 3 hours every Monday afternoon "tutoring" me in the wonders of physics.

Prior to taking physics, I had had relatively little difficulty understanding key concepts and general content of college entrance courses. However, physics was a conundrum. For the first time in my life, I knew the words the teacher was using made no sense.

So, every Monday afternoon when the other students had left for home due to early dismissal for religious education classes, Father Raymond would meet me in the physics lab and review the previous week's classes.

At times we would redo entire physics experiments, retracing electrical circuits, or measuring velocity and acceleration. Other times, detailed drawings on the board were needed to translate the specialized vocabulary into understandable component parts. Whatever assistance I needed, Father Raymond patiently gave.

I'll never forget the satisfaction and pleasure we both felt when I received the highest grade in the school on the New York State Regents examination. Our hours of work together had paid off, and I learned that at least one teacher really cared. I had learned never again to fear complexity and the unknown.

I Loved Mysteries

This concerns a teacher outside of the traditional classroom setting. I was considered handicapped by the state because of a very severe hearing loss. My parents found a certified teacher who was willing to work with me for $10.00 per hour. This was an unheard-of amount for tutoring back in 1950.

I like to hope that my speech improved as she put me through rigorous drills and constant repetitions of sounds that I myself could not hear or differentiate. But the lipreading seemed to me to get nowhere. Although she would select passages from books known to me, I became exceptionally frustrated trying to focus on each and every facial movement and have it all make sense.

Finally, one day as she was reading to me from a youthful mystery and my self-esteem was plummeting with my increasing frustration, she commented on how lipreading was a lot like detective work. I loved mysteries! Once she had my attention, she went on to relate lipreading to the detection process and she communicated to me that I need not grasp every word, but that I could rely on my own intelligence to fill in the gaps as long as I utilized all the "clues" available to me. This was a crucial turning point for me—not only in my progress in lip-reading but also in my acceptance of my handicap.

Although I do not remember her name, I still remember the sense of defeat lifting from my shoulders that afternoon. She would have a great laugh if she only knew some of the whacky answers that I have given, using my self-confidence and "guesses" as my guide!

A Role Model

I was a third grader and there was a Mrs. Hootin who was the person who made me decide that I wanted to be a teacher. The reason was twofold, I think, when I look back on it. Her room was always interesting. I went to elementary school in the early 50s, so you had to sit at a nailed or screwed-down desk. And the work we had to do was pretty rigid. But when your work was done, she had a science table with real things that you could feel and touch, and she had a social studies table and a reading corner. I think she was really kind of ahead of her time. I remember that about her.

Probably the most endearing part of my memory is that, when my mother was pregnant with my sister, Mrs. Hootin made such a big deal of it. She thought that was fabulous and she asked me every day about it. I even brought in a picture for her of my brother and me sitting on a couch, holding the new baby. She put it in the front of the room. I guess the whole thing was that the classroom was interested and she made me feel very special as an individual, very cared for, and a very important person in that classroom.

Anyhow, that's why I started to get the idea that I wanted to be a teacher even though I grew up in a family that really did not have the expectation for me, the daughter, to go to college and certainly did not have the money to do that. And when I met her, when I was a new teacher some 15 years later, at a corner bus stop, I realized that this was a "giant" of a person and she was about half as tall as I was. And that freaked me out because I thought, "My God, this was such a giant in my memory." I'll never forget her as long as I live.

An Invitation From a Second-Grade Teacher

What comes back very quickly is my second-grade teacher who invited me to learn to read. I was very bored with Dick and Jane or whoever it was at the time, and I was getting very antsy. She invited me to stay after school one day and introduced me to an orange book. I can't remember what the name of the orange book was, but I remember I read a book that had real words and didn't have big letters and big spaces in between. It had meaning and I got turned on to reading. As a result, every week I would stay after school a little bit and go in and she would give me another book to read. And for years, as a result, I had a relationship with this woman. When she stopped giving me books, she always invited me to talk about what I was reading. And it stayed with me so much that as an eighth grader I remember going back to see her.

The Math Teacher Taught Us Psychology

When I was in high school I remember one math teacher. I wasn't particularly interested in math at the time, but he was interested in us as students and how we developed. One particular thing that I remember is that a couple of times a week after class, for probably a semester, he taught us psychology from his experience when he had taken psychology as an undergraduate. That made a particular impact on me. There was a couple of us that he knew were interested in it. I felt personally taken care of.

A Very Tough Old Bird

In my junior year in high school there was a very tough old bird named Pearl Cord, who was probably not terribly old, probably about 40. But she was a very critical, demanding person with respect to writing. I remember she gave me a couple of books of A. E. Housman's poems and she thought I would enjoy reading them. And after a while, I did read them and they didn't really come through to me. I returned the books to her and I think she was disappointed that I didn't have much comment to make. At any rate, she encouraged me to submit a short story to a national school magazine and I did. I didn't think anything about it and one day, I think it was in an English class, the principal of the school came in and said that he had some pleasant news for us. I remember being totally taken aback when he said that he had just had word from the magazine that I had won the first prize on a short story. PS: A year later in college, I reread the Housman poems and found them absolutely wonderful and I still know pieces of them by heart.

A Special Sense of Myself

My homeroom teacher in fifth grade was also my math teacher and she and I got along well because I was a good math student. She was willing to show me algebra books that were seventh-grade material to try to challenge me. Sometimes, in free periods or at the end of the day or in homeroom, she would actually spend a little time with me, willing to challenge me on algebra. I think that was the first sort of academic "aha" experience that I had. I could do stuff that was not at the grade level that I was supposed to be on. I think that that encouragement was invaluable to me because I never felt uncomfortable in math until I got to graduate school, at which point I encountered all the real wizards and got put back in my place. But she gave me a special sense of myself academically that I never had before that time.

It Felt Good to Be Defended

When I was in junior high school, I was elected to the Honor Society and I can remember having worked with this one teacher. She was my English teacher, I think, for eighth grade. She was very nice. There were a number of us who had been elected to the Honor Society, the Junior Honor Society, I should say. So she decided that she was going to take a bunch of us that worked closely with her in one of the activities out for pizza. She was just a nice person. We all went out for pizza and one of the other girls who was with us made some kind of a comment to me to the effect of "Well, you were the last person who I thought would get into Junior Honor Society."

I think she had perceived herself as some kind of socially elite person and that I wasn't, and she couldn't see how I possibly could have gotten into this organization that now must be elite because she's in it. I was stunned. I had never had anybody speak to me quite like that. The teacher, without really being overpowering about it, came to my defense. I don't remember specifically what she said, but I remember feeling that she had come to my defense and that had an impact on me. I think, probably because I didn't have a terribly good self-concept, when somebody said something like that to me I really took it to heart and then when somebody came to my defense it felt good.

Being Physically or
Emotionally Abused

It would be nice if the only kinds of experiences that came to a person's mind as he or she reflected on having been in school were those that had positive emotional overtones. Sadly, though, such is not the case, although one could probably make the argument (one we do not support) that if school is preparation for life then it is not necessarily a bad thing that a youngster's school experiences include some of the bad along with the good. Regardless, if our own experiences in school, as well as those of any number of our friends and colleagues, are any measure, the point is a moot one. That is, negative memories of school abound.

It is true, although perhaps hard to believe, that there are adults among us whose most vivid memory of school is that of having been physically abused. "Hard to believe," that is, because we cannot link up the notion that a youngster can be in school and at the same time be physically abused by an adult. It is not supposed to happen, but on occasion it does. We have several examples of such occasions, and we expect they will make the reader wince as they made us wince.

There are also memories of a youngster who felt abused, not necessarily physically, but simply from being on the receiving end of adult indifference to pain, physical or psychological. It seems to be a condition that is the other side of the coin of

33

"Feeling Special in a Crowd," which was discussed in chapter 3. The point is that in some cases the behavior of an adult who is indifferent to a youngster's pain can be seen, in memory, as abusive.

A final point is in order in this introduction to chapter 5. The point also serves for chapters 6 and 7. Schools, like just about every other institution, are imperfect both in what they try to do and how they do it. This holds as well, we believe, for the people who work in them. Most principals and most teachers are sincere and sensitive people, but some are not. Most are not sadistic, but a few are. And there are certainly times when an otherwise warm and caring teacher or principal, for whatever reason, simply does not think about how his or her behavior will affect a child and behaves in a way that the child finds hurtful—and remembers for a long time.

He Growled and Walked Away

When I was in the seventh grade at Ingram Junior High School, I had the worst day of my life as a student, ever!

It was a frigid winter day and I was in gym class. I hated this class for two reasons. First, the gym teacher was an ex-marine and a harsh disciplinarian. Secondly, I was never very adept in gym. On this particular morning, the class was working on the parallel bars. There were two set up in the middle of the gym, with canvas mats below them. The gym teacher told us to get on the bars and to flip over. My turn came. The teacher was spotting at the other parallel bars. There was no one at mine. I flipped over and fell and hit my wrist on the metal base. I felt great pain and was dizzy. The teacher came over and began yelling at me for being clumsy. At this point, the 5-minute warning bell sounded and it was time to get changed. I went in the locker room and felt as if I was going to pass out. The teacher never once asked me how I was. In fact, he came in and continued to yell at me.

I left the gym and started to go to my next class when again I had the feeling of blacking out. I went directly to the nurse and she had me lie down. I told her about my fall from the bars. She examined my wrist and then told me I had broken it. The nurse called my mother at work. Mother had to take a taxi from work to school to pick me up and then go to the hospital. I was x-rayed, given an anesthetic, and the wrist fractures were set. I was sent home and did not return to school till a week later. My arm was in a cast and it was difficult to carry all my books. I went into gym with a great dread of seeing the gym teacher. He had absolutely no pity for me. Indeed, he yelled at me and wanted to know how long I had to have that "stupid cast on." I replied in a meek manner, "6 weeks." He growled and walked away.

What Were the Years of the Civil War?

I attended high school at a small boys' parochial boarding school in upstate New York. I was in the 11th-grade American History class with approximately 19 other students at the time this happened.

The teacher was a member of an order which originated in what we knew to be "French Canada." He, and all the other teachers in the school, wore an ankle-length black cassock, buttoned down the front.

The lesson, in my recollection, was progressing uneventfully. One student at a time was assigned to read aloud a section of a chapter in a paperback review book. The teacher periodically asked a question about the section which had just been read. He would then call the name of a specific student for an answer.

At one point, after one student read a paragraph, he asked, "What were the years, then, of the American Civil War?" He followed the question with the name, "Merrill?"

Some of us knew that Merrill had been talking with another student and had not been paying attention. "I don't know," he said. The teacher walked up the aisle and smacked him across the face with the back of his right hand. He was standing next to me. "You don't know because you weren't paying attention."

He then directed the student who had read the paragraph aloud to read it again. It was clear that the years were 1860 to 1865.

Merrill was asked again, "Now, what were the years of the Civil War?" He responded, "I don't know!" and then came another slap.

The sequence of events was repeated about three more times. Merrill ducked away from his slap and half rose from his seat. He was slapped again as the teacher lost his temper and began yelling, while swinging at the ducking student "1860 to 1865 . . . 1860 to 1865—say it—the years of the American Civil War were 1860 to 1865!" He had thrown the book down by now and he was swinging and slapping with both hands, not allowing Merrill the chance to speak or to rise from his seat.

I was terrified. I didn't know at the time why I was so fearful, and even now I don't quite understand my reaction of fear during the incident. I believe that I froze in a sort of time frame over that incident. The feeling of fear transferred to later classes. *I remember that I truly hated history as a subject after that time, and of being fearful when I was required to remember dates or recount historical chronology.* I carried this feeling through later years and, quite frankly, I still experience that feeling when I am asked the date of an historical event that I should know.

I can say one thing, however, I have never forgotten that the American Civil War was fought between the years 1860 to 1865!

I Cried All the Way to Her Office

I was 7 years old and in third grade. The principal would let us play in the gym while she ate her lunch there. This hour was considered our recess. One day, I felt I had something crucial to tell one of my friends who was clear across the gym. As I was running over to her, another girl accidentally ran into me. I went crashing into the bench along the wall and then fell to the floor, where I started to scream from the pain in my right leg. The principal came over to me and ordered me to get up and to stop screaming. The screaming stopped but the pain did not, and I could not get up. I told the principal that my leg hurt and that I couldn't stand up, so she yanked me up. Once I was up, she ordered me to walk, which was out of the question since I was only standing on one leg, and the other would not support me, not to mention the pain coming from it. She yelled at me again to walk, so I had to try, but I started screaming again from the pain. She kept making me try to walk, and I was so afraid of this woman at this point that I really had no choice. She told me to walk straight to her office so that she could call my mother. I thought I was going to get in trouble for running in the gym. I limped down the hall. My leg wouldn't really work no matter how hard I tried. I cried all the way to her office, more because I was afraid of this woman and less because of the pain. My mother came to get me and later that day took me to the hospital where they informed us that my right leg was broken.

I Was Quickly Reduced to Tears

It was April of my senior year in high school. An English teacher was in charge of the senior class and had been forever. It was a small school and I was class president in both my junior and senior years. This teacher and I had bucked heads on some issues. I don't know if I truly recognized it at the time, though I can now, but it was as though I was trying to claim my independence and she was trying to keep me from doing that. Also, I had her as a teacher when I was a junior. I always felt some kind of estrangement between us.

She was an active member of the Teachers Association and they had a scholarship for kids who wanted to be teachers. My biology teacher had asked me if I had applied. I think I was probably reluctant because it meant I had to go through the English teacher. Anyhow, at my biology teacher's urging, I did. I came into school one day and I went to her homeroom and asked her for the application papers. She literally threw them at me and they landed on the floor. She said, "You're wasting your time if you think you're a candidate for the scholarship."

I was really surprised because I wasn't a bad student. I did quite well academically. I'd been a student leader, very involved, but I knew that for whatever reason she didn't like me. I guess it was mutual.

Anyway, I knelt down, picked up the application, and got out of the room. Of course, I didn't cry while I was in the room, but I was quickly reduced to tears when I got outside. I went down to the biology teacher and he could see how upset I was. He said, "What's wrong?" I said, "Aw, she threw the paper at me and told me not to waste my time."

The nice part of this story is that he sat me down and said, "You will fill this out," and he sat there with me while I did just that and he said, "Give it to me. I'll turn it in." I was so relieved to think I didn't have to go back to her and I was sure I didn't stand a chance of getting the scholarship. The truth was that I did need the money. I can't say I didn't care.

The really surprising thing about this was that at graduation I was sitting there listening to speeches and somebody nudged me and said, "Nancy, that's you." I said, "What?" and lo and behold, I had won that scholarship. I hate to say this, but even into my very adult years, I have always wanted her to know that the scholarship didn't go to waste. I did become a teacher and a good one. I know that I should have different feelings as an adult, but that's something I've never worked out. I've always resented that woman for the way she treated me. At a 25th class reunion a few years ago, she was there. I was civil to her, smiled, but I really wanted to tell her off.

You're All the Same, All of You

This was in the eighth grade. At first it involved me, another student, and my science teacher. Later, my parents, all the other students in class, and the school board were brought into the picture.

One day when class was in session, a student named Sissie came in a bit late. The teacher was in front of the room and out of his mouth came, "You're all the same, all of you." There was a hush that was deafening, and at that point my insides began to race. Sissie was Jewish, and everyone knew what the teacher was saying. I just sat there and stared.

Sissie got very upset and left the room. At this time, the teacher looked at me and said, "That's right, you're all the same. The whole bunch of you." I exploded and ran out of the room. Sissie and I both went to the principal's office and told him what had happened. He said he would help us iron out the problem.

Our parents were outraged. They demanded that something be done to rectify the situation. All of our classmates were asked to write down in their own words what had happened in class that day. Sissie and I had already been transferred into another science class. Being in another class was somewhat of a relief, but at the same time my feelings were very mixed up. The turmoil between me and my other classmates really shook me. It seemed that being Jewish was an oddity and also capable of causing problems.

As the situation developed, my and Sissie's parents wanted the teacher dismissed from his job. They appeared to be on a personal vendetta. She and I kind of got lost in the whole mess. It was as if the parents were the injured parties, not us.

The depositions from our classmates were mixed. Some had heard what we heard. Others said they weren't sure what happened. The principal had waited a few days to get the depositions, and as a result, memories were cloudy. A school board meeting was called and both sets of parents attended. Again, the two of us were not involved. The feeling of lack of control on my part hit again.

The outcome was that Sissie and I stayed in our new classroom and the teacher kept his job. By the time it was over I was very worn out and confused. I do know that I felt very incomplete in my experience of the event. The process lasted approximately 3 weeks.

The irony of this is that in the 11th grade I walked into my first chemistry class and guess who was the instructor? I couldn't believe my eyes! Somehow I ended up in his class. This sent my head swimming back to 8th grade, and I felt the same hurts I had felt back then. Needless to say I transferred out immediately.

I'll Walk Sideways Again

September 1962, the first day of school for the incoming class of freshmen at Albany Prep, a Catholic high school for boys. Admission to this school was competitive; the applicants, who came from all over the metropolitan area, had to take a test. The school and its teachers had a reputation for being extremely strict and disciplined. This was the first day of school only for the new freshmen. Upper classmen would start the next day.

There were slightly over 200 young men, dressed in jackets, ties, and with very short haircuts, standing in the school gym on what I remember as a hot morning. Although very few of us knew anyone else, there was the expected amount of small talk. There was also a little bit of low-key horsing around.

Fr. Robert Intell entered the gym and stood with his hands tucked into a sash that was tied around a long black robe. I clearly remember that he stood there for a brief period of time and then, in a regular conversational tone, said, "Quiet."

Fr. Intell's position in the administration at the school was analogous to that of a vice principal. However, his title was Dean of Discipline. He was every bit as impressive as his title. Of course, I was only 14 and had been taught by nuns for the previous 8 years, but "Bobby" looked to be the biggest and certainly the most intimidating person I have ever seen before or since.

After he said, "Quiet," everybody was quiet. Then he just stood there and waited. As might be expected with a gym filled with nervous adolescent boys, somebody said something to the kid next to him. I'm not sure how long it took, but it happened.

Fr. Intell took that God-given opportunity to quite simply beat the shit out of the boy, up and down the gym, right there in front of everybody.

I now know that experience to be a near perfect demonstration of one-trial learning. For the next 4 years I walked sideways when I saw him in the hall. This year is my 25th reunion. I'll walk sideways again.

She Pulled the Pencil Out of My Left Hand

When I was in the first grade, I have a vivid recollection of the teacher pulling the pencil out of my left hand as she was teaching us how to write. She pushed it into my right hand, stood over me, shook her finger and scolded, "You must learn to write with your right hand. We live in a right-handed world and left-handed people are cripples in today's world. You must write with your right hand." And I remember feeling very frustrated and angry about it because, although I was somewhat ambidextrous and there were many things that I did with my left hand or my right hand, my inclination was to write with my left hand.

I was terrified not to write with my right hand. I was going to be handicapped in all the world if I didn't. My handwriting is terrible to this day and it is because I was forced to write with my right hand, but my natural inclination was to use my left.

Knocked Their Heads Together

My sixth-grade teacher was about 6'4" and short of temper. One day, two of the boys had a fight while he was out of the room. We knew he would never tolerate it. He came back in the middle of this fight and took those kids, lifted them bodily, one in each hand, knocked their heads together, sat them down, and then proceeded to systematically empty their desks of everything in them. Then he threw it all the full length of the room, against the wall, right over my head. I was sitting in the back. And for 5 minutes I was bombarded by these missiles, scared stiff. I had no idea what was going to happen. When it was all over, I, being a polite young person and well trained by my mother, saw this mess on the floor so I got up and started picking it up. He said, "Al, sit down! Sit right there!" So this pile of junk was laying there, for a day or two. He was making a fool of himself, really. But this was his way of quelling a riot. It's like these people who kill for peace.

Tricycle Trauma

During kindergarten recess, I watched as a little girl rode round and round the room on a shiny red tricycle. How I waited for a turn! Then, as I rounded my second lap on that tricycle, the clang clang of the bell sounded to end recess. Obediently, I hopped off, wheeled the trike to an out-of-the-way place, and returned to my seat. As I eagerly awaited our next activity, I saw the look of displeasure on the teacher's face. I watched, unsuspectingly, as she marched over to *me*. I was horrified. I had returned the tricycle to the wrong place. I was on the verge of tears. Where did it belong? I wheeled it from one place to the next. I just didn't know. Her stare grew angrier. Her voice grew louder. Everyone was tssk-tssking. Finally, little Johnny Farfel received a smile and nod of approval when he wheeled that trike to its "proper" place. You can believe that not once did I ever attempt to ride that tricycle again!

Sometimes I wonder how many good times I did without, fearful of that disapproving glare or snide remark? Occasionally, I remember those days and reflect upon my own teaching. I only hope I have never left a mark on one of my students like the one that teacher left on me, unknowingly, unthinkingly, I'm sure, that one kindergarten afternoon.

He Had a Great Arm

I was a freshman in high school, an all-boys high school on the south side of the city. My gym class was sort of like military training. The gym teacher was at one time a Big Eight quarterback and in 1959 he took his team to a bowl game. One of the ways you had to exit the gym if you were in the last class of the day was something that he called the Polish Crawl. We all had to line up along the width of the gym, and everybody had to crawl out on their shirt and your shirt would then clean the floor. He would stand on the stage, which was directly across from the line, and if you got up too high and you weren't crawling he would throw a red hard rubber ball at you with tremendous speed. He could really cause pain. Yeah, he was devastating. He had a great arm and he would do that. He not only would hit you but then he would make you go back to do it again. Then you would have to do it more quickly because if you didn't move out quickly you were late for your homeroom and then you got detention.

Being Different—A WASP in South Boston

I was raised in South Boston, which is essentially Irish-Catholic, but my family was very Waspish. We were very definitely a minority family. The school system was set up so that you started Kindergarten at age 4 1/2. That's very young. This classroom was filled with the Muldoons, the Delaneys, and the O'Haras—and the teacher is Miss O'Rourke. And there's this kid, me, with this funny name, Melvin Peter, who becomes sort of like a symbol for all that's ill in the world—this little kid. So anyway, this teacher really did not like me. Can you imagine—at 4 1/2!

It was brought up a number of times that I had a funny first name and that I was very, very different. I was sort of segregated. I was shunted off to one side of the classroom and I was always working alone. I never could really understand why, but I was. But anyway, it all came to a head one day when the teacher decided that we were going to make placemats for our mothers. First came the colored piece of paper, and then she explained how to fringe with a pair of scissors. I don't know why, but I didn't understand what fringing was all about and that you only snipped an inch in. I snipped all the way across the paper so that I was almost to the other side. I suppose I realized there was something amiss and I really shouldn't cut all the way, so that I wouldn't then have two pieces of paper. Anyhow, now I have this colored piece of paper that was to be a placemat and I really didn't understand what that was. In addition, I had cut all the way across. And the teacher saw that. She grabbed me, the boy who was taller than everybody else and, making things worse, with the funny first name. She held me up to ridicule in front of the class to show the stupid piece of work that I had done. And she said something about my name. I really can't remember what it was. Then she took me to the principal who was Miss Murray (a good Irish name) and told the principal that this is the type of work that we get from his kind.

Both of them yelled at me and wagged their fingers at me. That's all that happened, but then I was sent back to the classroom. The funniest thing about it was that I was used to that. I felt unhappy and I felt very alone, and I felt there was something different about me that nobody liked. But it was probably about 15 years later before I cried about it, because I never understood what it was all about. So then after my wife and I were married for a couple of years, one night we were talking late at night in bed and I told her this story. You know, I said, "I couldn't believe. . . ."

She Doesn't Have Any Nails, Anyhow

From as far back as I can remember I bit my fingernails. No amount of threatening or punishment from my parents could cure the habit. Then, in my junior year of high school, I had a teacher for shorthand and transcription who insisted that the nails should not be seen over the tips of your fingers and once a week she made a check of everyone in the class. If your nails were too long to suit her, you were told to cut them overnight or she would do it the next day—and on occasion she did. After 3 or 4 weeks, she started making cracks like "I don't need to check Mary, she doesn't have any nails anyhow." Needless to say, being the perverse person that I am, I decided to let my nails grow. After much work on my part, she finally noticed that indeed my nails were now showing over my fingertips and I was treated not only to a sarcastic comment but to the usual order to cut them by the next day or she would do it for me. The next day I came to class with my "long" nails and when she did her inspection, with clippers in hand, I sat on my hands and would not let her cut them. A verbal battle ensued in which she stated that I knew the rules and I stated that until my grades were affected by them they stayed. All this resulted in my first and only visit to the principal (who was not overly concerned with the whole matter and told me to return to class the next day—nails intact).

The Scariest Thing

I was in the first grade. I had my hand out in the aisle. It was a game that all the kids would play at lavatory time. We would try and catch someone coming down the aisle. It was strictly forbidden, and the idea was to do it without being caught by the teacher. Well, she caught me. She came flying down the aisle, grabbed me by the arm, and spanked me. Then she made me stand in the corner in a trash can for the rest of the day. I was scared. It stayed with me a long time, all through school. I would say it's the scariest thing that ever happened to me in school.

6

Being Embarrassed

Embarrassing moments, it seems, are not in short supply in the lives of schoolchildren. Many of the narratives we received describe such conditions. Sometimes, it appears that what occurred was inadvertent. Something just happened, with no one's ill intent, that resulted in a youngster's feeling ill at ease or publicly ridiculed. Other times, the sense of embarrassment resulted from what seemed to have been deliberate actions taken by an adult or another student or students, again publicly.

It is, of course, the public or semipublic nature of the circumstance that is the critical thing. For example, a teacher can talk to a youngster in private about being obese and that youngster may well feel uncomfortable. However, at the least, the discomfort is private. On the other hand, it is a different story when comments about a pupil's weight are made publicly and one's warts are made visible for all to see and laugh at. The same condition would hold if a teacher, in private conference with a student, continued to press him or her for answers to questions to which he or she could not respond correctly. Feelings of discomfort would most likely develop, but not for the "world" to bear witness.

Why, though, are there so many of these quick recalls of embarrassing situations, and why do they occur in the first place? We can only speculate, of course. It may be the case, relative to the quickness and volume of recall, that feelings of having been embarrassed, private as they are, simply stay buried until some point in time, a precious moment, when they may be talked about with ease. They may smoulder for years just waiting for a little fresh fuel to be thrown on the coals. And the question, "What is your most vivid recollection?" may be that fuel.

The second question—"Why do these situations occur?"— requires a different answer. First, as we noted, sometimes embarrassing circumstances simply happen: an answer to a question that strikes others as funny and they laugh, or being unable to wait till recess to go to the bathroom and wetting one's pants. On the other hand, and this may be a way to understand (but not necessarily accept) deliberately provoking embarrassment— a teacher may hold to the idea that embarrassing a pupil is a relatively benign way to get that pupil to change his or her behavior. From the reactions we received, though, and as the reader will discover, teachers who hold this point of view are more successful at encouraging student resentment than at changing behavior. Another thought occurs to us about the high incidence of embarrassing moments (at least in recall) connected with the way schoolwork is conceived. It is that there is an element of students having to give a performance daily (as do teachers), almost as though they are on stage. The problem is, to continue the metaphor, there is not too much time for rehearsal and, thus, some of these performances are likely to have mistakes and therefore be embarrassing. We suspect that one or more of these memories will resonate with most readers.

The Entire Class Knew

All through elementary school, I was a fat kid and I was made to feel like an outcast because of my size. I was always made fun of and called names. In fourth grade, I remember one day wearing brown and white checkered polyester pants, and an off-white turtleneck which stretched down to my knees. While I was sitting with a group of classmates, the one boy I never liked told me I had a hole in my pants and, of course, I didn't believe him. He was always making me feel rotten. Finally, it got around the group and the nosey girl in the class, who unfortunately was sitting with me, went up and told the teacher. I wasn't aware of it until Mrs. McGuire came over and asked me to stand up so she could see the hole in my pants. I was so embarrassed because now the entire class knew, especially the boy I had a bad crush on. They were all laughing even though I refused to stand up and show the teacher.

A Hell of a Way to Teach

I remember in second grade having to stay after school to do my homework because I wasn't grasping some concepts in reading. I remember just being very angry and upset about that. Well, I think it was embarrassing that it happened to me. And I think I came away from that—not exactly at that time, but later—thinking that making someone stay after school was a hell of a way to teach.

Well, Come On, You Should Know That

This is no specific incident. But it is sort of a collection of memories of being called on and being embarrassed by not being able to answer a question. When a particular teacher would ask me, I would fumble around for an answer and get very impatient with myself because I didn't know it. But I didn't know how to respond to my not knowing. I felt embarrassed about it, with the teacher pushing on me with the sense of "Well, come on, you should know that." I was in high school, a sophomore, and it was a very sensitive age. And I didn't think I could meet the teacher's expectations for performance, even though I was a better-than-average student. And as I look back, even though I learned to respect the teacher, I had some really rough moments and was really stressed initially with feeling that sense of embarrassment.

You Can Just Imagine How I Felt

This was fourth grade. They had monitors to watch the boys and girls when they went to the bathroom. This day it was my turn. I stood by the door and waited for all the girls to take their turns. I was having a terrible time because I had to go to the bathroom, but I didn't say anything. I wet my pants. The teacher kept it very secret, took care of the whole thing, and told me to go back to my seat and everything was taken care of. You can just imagine how I felt.

All I Expected Was a Lecture

In all my years of school, one experience that I will never forget is the time I got caught for passing a note to a friend. Although this may seem to be a very ordinary situation, at the time in my life it made a strong impression on me.

I was in sixth grade at the time and very preoccupied with friends and the social interactions of school. I remember that before school I received some very important news which I just had to tell my best friend, Kate. Because this information could not wait until lunch, I wrote a note during homeroom which I gave to Kate before the first class began. Although I knew that writing notes during class was wrong and if caught I would be punished, it seemed okay to pass one before class without disrupting anyone. Unfortunately, the note did cause problems because Kate shared my note with another friend, Stacy, and they were not so cautious. Without my knowing it, the note that I had written was passed in the middle of their math class. Even though I was not in the room, my name was on the note and all three of us got in trouble.

I had never gotten in trouble before, but for a first offense of note passing I expected a lecture from the teacher or, at worst, having to stay inside for recess. The teacher, on the other hand, had previous problems with students passing notes and decided to make an example of us. That afternoon I alone was called to the principal's office, something which was very embarrassing for me. After telling me how disappointed he was with me, Mr. Johnson returned my note to me and informed me that copies of it would be sent home to each of our parents. I was devastated; not only was I singled out to be reprimanded by the principal, but I also discovered that my personal note was xeroxed and would be read by my parents as well as Stacy's and Kate's.

The next day, my mother and I sat down to talk about what had happened. My parents had received the note along with a letter from the teacher emphasizing the severity of note passing in school and the need for strict punishment for this act. I was ready to defend myself. However, my mother needed no explanation and in fact dismissed the note as something typical at my age. She was upset that the teacher could xerox something that was intended to be kept private. For the first time since the note was intercepted, I stopped being afraid long enough to realize that in a small way my personal rights had been violated.

A few days later, the teacher stopped me in the hall to ask why my parents hadn't signed and returned the letter when both Kate and Stacy's parents had. I told him that my mother didn't sign it because we wanted to come in and talk to him about it in person. The teacher then asked whether or not I had really taken it home to them. I was so humiliated; now the teacher was practically accusing me of not taking the letter home and of lying to him. I felt my face grow warm and tears form in my eyes.

I learned a lot from this experience. Not only was it the first time I got in trouble at school but it also showed me how it feels to have a teacher accuse me of lying. I had let myself be intimidated by an authority figure without realizing that, although I was a child and had made a mistake, he still had no right to xerox my note.

Self-Conscious About My Handwriting

My teacher in third grade was Miss McStample. I remember her as a solidly stout, severe woman with dark hair pulled back smoothly into a bun. We must have been getting ready to learn cursive writing because she would make us do what seemed to me to be endless writing exercises. These exercises consisted of writing row after row of very narrowly spaced, slightly slanted connecting straight lines, alternating with row after row of very narrowly spaced slightly slanted connecting circles.

The examples of slanted lines and circles that Miss McStample wrote on the blackboard were marvels to me. Each was perfectly even, perfectly spaced, exactly precise.

The other kids in the class, it seemed to me and apparently to her, were able to do reasonable facsimiles of her perfect examples. I was not. No matter how hard I tried, I just couldn't do it. I was very self-conscious about my messy lines and circles.

One day, Miss McStample made me stay in while everyone else went outside for recess. She stood over me and made me do slanted lines and circles. I felt awful. With her watching, I did them even less well and I could feel her displeasure. This is a very vivid memory for me.

There is no punch line to the story. To this day, I am very self-conscious about my handwriting and consider it to be messy and unattractive. I attribute this self-consciousness to that experience with Miss McStample.

She Was Going to Whip Me Into Line

In the third grade, I had a witch named Mrs. Patterlo who had it in her mind that she was going to whip me into line. I was a dreamer and a goof-off. School bored me terribly. I would rather be reading at home, at the library, anywhere but in her classroom.

Our assignment one day was to use the list of spelling words to construct a little story. I just didn't feel like doing it.

While the rest of the group wrote, I sat and daydreamed. I claimed I couldn't think of anything to write. Mrs. Patterlo's response was to take the list of words down the hall to the second-grade class and ask four of them to write stories with the list. I remember vividly the sick feeling of humiliation when those four second graders, one of whom was a good friend, came into our room to read their stories out loud in front of the class. Mrs. Patterlo went on and on about how shameful it was that I couldn't do this when these "little kids" were capable of completing the assignment. I remember wanting to crawl under my desk. The whole class was snickering at me.

Her motive, I suppose, was to goad me into "performing." But I think it simply made me resentful. I became angry at school. In several more years, I knew I wanted to be a teacher and I vowed I would never humiliate any kid in my class.

This Is What a Slob Is

I know generally I had no respect for my instructors in elementary school. I know specifically in second grade I hated my instructor. It seems like she was always knocking me personally because of my weight problem back then.

I was very big. My nickname was Bubbles. Fighting words, fighting. And she used to say to me all the time, "You should really lose a lot of weight." I guess I was kind of messy, too. And she would also gather all the students in the class, have them stand around my desk, have me open it up, and say, "This is what a slob is." I also had a nervous habit of biting my nails and she said, "Your nails are too short. Quit biting them. That's stupid." And she always criticized me a lot. She also criticized another fat kid. There were two really fat kids. Two Bubbles. I used to get in fights because of my weight. And I was the one who was always punished. Some people naturally look down on fat people and they're not considered on the same plane. I always thought she just didn't like the way I looked and that she wanted to humiliate me so much that I would lose weight.

I Had to Wet My Pants Before I Could Get the
Teacher to Believe Me

It was after 2 o'clock in the afternoon. We had just returned from recess and Mrs. Wellington, my third-grade teacher, was working with students in math over in the corner near the flower boxes. I was busy doing my seat work, when suddenly I had the urge to go to the bathroom.

Now, Mrs. Wellington had many rules. One of the rules was that, if a student wanted to use the bathroom or get a drink of water, you were only allowed to do so at lunch time or recess time. You were not allowed to do so at any other time of the day unless you had a note from your parents that said you had a problem and needed to use the bathroom more frequently or needed a drink of water more often for medical reasons.

Well, I wasn't one of those kids with a note. What could I do? I crossed my legs, pushed down hard in my chair, prayed to God for this urge to go away. It persisted. Finally, I raised my hand. After a few minutes of trying to get Mrs. Wellington's attention, I succeeded. She asked me what I wanted. I responded with "Mrs. Wellington, may I go to the bathroom?" She peered at me over her spectacles, which were strategically placed on the tip end of what appeared to be a very long pointed nose, and said sternly, "Now you know the rules, you should have used the bathroom during lunch or recess time. You'll have to wait until school is over for the day. Be quiet and do your work!"

Needless to say, I thought my bladder would burst. I started telling the kids around me that I really had to go to the bathroom. Joey, who was always getting into trouble with Mrs. Wellington, advised me by saying "Get up and go. Don't listen to her. If ya gotta go, ya gotta go." Well, I just couldn't do that. I would be disobeying one of the rules and I'd get into a lot of trouble. Finally, my best friend, Karen, raised her hand and told Mrs. Wellington that this was an emergency and her best friend, meaning me, really had to go or she (meaning me) was going to wet her pants. Well, Mrs. Wellington really became angry and sounded even more agitated than before. She told me I was disrupting the class and if I did not stop I would be punished.

I put my head down and tried not to show anyone that I was crying. I wasn't the kind of kid who caused trouble. I was trying to control my emotional feelings and my physical feelings all at the same time. I couldn't understand why my teacher was being so strict. Couldn't she make an exception? This was an emergency. All that kept going through my mind was, "What would the other kids think of me if I wet my pants? What would Mrs. Wellington do to me?"

Well, to make an agonizing story short, I did wet my pants. I couldn't help it. All the kids around me saw the puddle under my seat as they left the classroom that day. Not one of them ever teased me. Mrs. Wellington came over to me after everyone had gone. Of course, I remained seated. I was too mortified to move. She looked at me, saw the puddle, and said, "Oh dear, you had an accident. I guess you really did have to go to the bathroom! Don't worry, I'll get the custodian to clean this up. You run along now." With that, I flew out of the classroom and ran all the way home.

Just think! I had to wet my pants to get the teacher to believe me! Rules, rules, rules, aren't there ever any exceptions? Or is it like Joey said, "When ya gotta go, ya gotta go"?

Put Your Gum on the End of Your Nose

My first year at Blue Hill Central School was fourth grade. It was the first place where I had to ride a school bus to school. The first time I was caught chewing gum in school, it was quite a shock to hear the teacher tell me to put my gum on the end of my nose and leave it there until I got home. When I got on the school bus, the first thing I did was to remove the gum. The bus driver stopped the bus and informed me that I was to put the gum back on my nose and leave it there. I remember that I never got "caught" chewing gum again. You just know that I was embarrassed but my self-esteem was left intact.

I Was Found Guilty

One of the most vivid memories I have of school was when I was in the fourth grade. Our teacher, Mrs. Kankowski, would take away students' chairs when they talked out of turn. Needless to say, one morning I was found guilty and I was asked to stand at my desk for the rest of the day. I remember being very embarrassed and humiliated because, in general, I was a pretty good kid. After about an hour or so, my nose started to bleed. I was sent to the nurse and then sent home, luckily for me!

The Red Barn, My Foot

When I was in first grade, we were sitting in a group reading circle and it was my turn to read. I read something that wasn't on the page and I can remember my teacher saying, "The red barn, my foot." I didn't understand the expression so I just kept looking at the page looking for where it said, "The red barn, my foot." And I just kept looking at it and I just didn't know what to say at all. So I sat there really, really embarrassed.

I Had My Eyes Closed for a Second

I had a history teacher for a couple of years. He taught humanities and a general arts kind of class. His name was Marty Felton. He collected little British roadsters and always wore Harris tweeds and an ascot and big clunky English shoes. The first class that I had him for was a world history class and I sat in the back row. It was my first class in the morning and I wasn't always real alert. This one morning I must have had my eyes closed for a second, when I noticed the class was real quiet. Just as I looked up I saw his hand about 5 feet away, in the process of lobbing a piece of chalk through the air into my face. That was his way of getting my attention. He made a public example of me.

I Can Remember Feeling Awful

I think this is the first time I ever remember having been embarrassed. I was in the sixth grade back in Edwards School in Meriden, Connecticut. And that was kind of a long time ago. It must have been 1933 or 34. I even remember the teacher's name. It was Miss Wintell. We were somehow studying something about Yale University because that is in Connecticut. And we had to do projects and I did mine with a picture of a castle on a mountain with kind of a path going up the mountain. I can remember I made one of those S-shaped paths and it was like going up a mountain and I put vertical lines in to indicate the sheerness of the path. What I was doing was indicating on the path the years that Yale University had expanded and added this program and that program, and this department and that department. It must have taken me several days to do it all. And I finished it and the teacher thought it was simply not a very creative or worthwhile thing, and she let me know it and she let the rest of the class know it. I can remember feeling awful about that.

A Short Artistic Career

When I was in third grade, my teacher gave us the homework assignment of drawing a picture of our house. It was a Friday night and the picture had to be handed in on Monday morning. She gave each one of us the approved piece of paper to use for our drawing.

In my family, Friday night meant dinner at my grandparents' house. Also, in my family, the rule was that homework had to be done on Friday and couldn't be left until Sunday. My brother and I would bring our books to my grandparents' house and do our work while my grandmother, mother, and great aunt would do the dishes. I remember hoping for homework, since doing the dishes was one of my most hated tasks.

This Friday night, I sat down to draw my house and realized that I didn't have a great memory for what it actually looked like. First I drew the picture on one side of the paper. The house didn't look right, so I turned the paper over and drew it again on the other side. The picture still didn't look right, but I had used up both sides of the approved piece of paper. I put it in my folder and decided to hand it in the way it was. My mother assured me that I had nothing to worry about, since these pictures were being done by third graders. How good did the teacher think they were going to be?

On Monday morning, I handed in my house picture along with the other students in the class. On Tuesday morning, we arrived at school to find that our teacher had set up a bulletin board with all the pictures. My house looked terrible. The peaked roof lines didn't meet but crisscrossed each other. Some of the students in the class asked me if I lived in a windmill. I had to admit that it did resemble a windmill quite a bit. The picture that drew the most praise was a professional-looking drawing of my best friend's house, complete with a car sitting in the driveway. When asked how she did it, she told us that her father (who owned a furniture store) had his graphic artist do the picture. She proudly admitted that she colored in the garage windows. I felt confident that the teacher would berate her for not following directions. Also, her picture was not on the approved piece of paper. Instead, she pointed out that picture to the whole class as a beautiful example of a picture of a house. My picture was pointed out as an example of a sloppy picture. I was terribly embarrassed, especially when the whole class laughed.

Experiencing Injustice

Schools, like any other social system, have rules about the behavior of people in them. Some of these rules are officially codified and some are developed, it seems, at the whim of an individual teacher or other adult. Although most youngsters would probably say that there are too many of them, without rules (or at least some rules) the system would break down.

Where there are rules, of course, there must be people to enforce them, and so we are led to the question of How the rule system is enforced in schools. Put another way, How is the administration of school justice played out? Who does what and how?

People who work in the schools play what seems to be, on the face of it, an incompatible set of roles where matters of rule breaking are concerned. In metaphorical terms, teachers and principals can become arresting officers, detectives, judges, and juries. One person may play all these roles at pretty much the same time, or they may be split between teacher and principal. For example, a teacher may discover a rule has been broken, investigate the transgression, declare a student or students guilty, and set a sentence detention for 3 days. Or a teacher may decide a rule has been broken, but the nature of the infraction—fighting, for instance—requires that the combatants be sent to the principal's office. The principal then assumes the role of detective, tries to unravel the circumstances that led to the fight, makes a guilty or not-guilty determination, and imposes a sentence if that is required.

Although most of the time this process works well enough, most principals or teachers will probably say that its implementation takes too much of their time. More important, however, is that even though a youngster may be punished for breaking a rule, there tend to be few complaints if the process is seen as having been carried out with fairness. Kids are likely to take their "medicine" without complaint as long as they think that justice has been administered with equity.

In the great majority of instances, our sense of what happens is that there is fairness in how principals and teachers approach this part of their job. We have observed a principal, for example, patiently unraveling the circumstances of a fight so that when a decision was made there was no dispute that it was not a fair one. Also, we think this type of situation is repeated many times during a school day. There are times, however, when—for whatever reason—a teacher or a principal behaves capriciously with regard to an offense. A teacher with a particularly sensitive nerve about certain types of student misbehavior overreacts when that nerve is touched and makes decisions that are seen as unjust. Or a principal who is over his or her head with other demands neglects to listen to both sides of a particular story and renders a verdict that is perceived as unfair.

One thing we know, then (and the memories in this chapter make our knowledge ever more clear), is that youngsters have a highly refined sense of justice and are capable of long-remembered anger or indignation over a situation when they feel they have been treated unjustly. At least, this is the major message of this chapter. Memories of having been dealt with in an unjust manner linger a long time. One of the present authors, for example, recalls an incident in high school some 50 years ago of having been singled out by a teacher and then punished for talking when no talking had occurred. There was no appeal and the memory and resentment still exist.

Why the administration of injustice, as it were? Surely the adults who work in our schools are not unjust people. We suspect that what happens in many cases is that teachers or principals sometimes simply become overwhelmed with demands on their time and competency. A pupil does something at precisely the wrong moment—the proverbial backbreaking straw—and is dealt with in an unjust manner: not listened to, not believed when he or she is telling the truth, or simply overreacted to. And obviously, all of this is most likely to happen if the pupil has a "bad actor" history.

There are, of course, other reasons that pupils experience injustice in school. For example, it is no secret that school principals are under great pressure to support a teacher, even when they know that teacher has been wrong in a decision or accusation. And certainly teachers and principals mete out injustice when they feel pressure not to violate one policy or another. Regardless, as we suggested earlier, it may be that memories of having been treated unjustly stay with adults longer than do most other memories. These memories, in a way, are scars that do not heal very quickly or very well.

Through the Eye of the Beholder

It was recess in the fifth grade. A few classes were out on the playground as well as ours. Everyone was running around having a wonderful time. With all the fun going on I wanted to get my share. I picked up a ball, usually used for dodge ball, and threw it at a kid. I thought I knew him well enough to do this and start some fun. Evidently, I was quite wrong. He (Bobby) became rather upset and started hitting me. Our teacher noticed it right away and grabbed both of us by the arms very tightly. What she said then was probably the worst thing to ever happen to me. "You two are going to the principal's office!" I was so scared. I had never been there for anything bad before and I knew I didn't want to go there now. I told my teacher that Bobby just started hitting me. She calmly explained to me that she knew that but she couldn't take just one of us. This was nice to hear but had little effect on my nervousness about seeing the principal.

As we stood in the office in front of a short but fat man with a mustache, one hand on his chin, and his eyes digging into the both of us, I started to cry. He didn't seem too sympathetic to me as he had both of us explain our sides of the story. As they were told, all three of us began to understand what a misunderstanding the whole thing was. It seemed that Bobby thought that I had thrown the ball to purposely start a fight. Now that he understood, I understood, and Mr. C. understood. We were to simply shake hands and not to let it happen again. What a relief!

No Way to Begin School

The first part of the first grade we moved to a new school on the other side of Cincinnati. I had an older sister, 6 years older, and she was in the seventh grade. On the first day of school, there was something that she had that I needed to have, so I had to go up to the second floor, which was where all upper grades were. I remember meeting a woman. Her name was Miss Williams and she looked like a bulldog. As a matter of fact, she did have a Boston bulldog. She was the eighth-grade teacher. She said, "What are you doing up on this floor! First graders are little and they are not allowed to be here. You're only allowed to be downstairs." I tried to explain that I needed to see my sister who was up there but that wasn't good enough a reason. She sent me back downstairs. I felt mortified and resentful because I knew I had a good reason, but she was a teacher and I had to do what she said. So I felt like I was just squashed, not treated justly, and it was no way to begin school.

Who Is Pauly Wally?

This was in the eighth grade and it is one of my most vivid memories from school. This was the time when Beatlemania was going through the United States. There was a group of us in class that were real Beatle freaks. We ate, drank, and slept

Beatles. We would bring pictures to school to show them off and trade them. In the schoolyard one day, we were trading and we had a real good crop of Paul McCartney pictures. Recess was over but we hadn't finished trading yet and people hadn't finished looking at them. So when we went into class, I started passing a note around saying that I would like such and such a picture, or whatever. We were passing the pictures around while the teacher was teaching. Eventually, she caught the note en route somewhere. She had the note passer come up and she took it and read it. "Where are the pictures of my Pauly Wally?" it said. So I slunk down in the chair and she said, "Who is Pauly Wally and who is this note going to? Who wrote this note?" So I stood up and she said, "OK, and this is going to whom?" "OK, you stand up." So she had all of us involved eventually standing up. "Who is Pauly Wally?" Everybody was laughing. "Well, he's one of the Beatles." "Oh, and who has the pictures?" "I really don't know." No one would say a word. "Who has the pictures?" "I'm not sure who has the pictures." Finally, she got around to whoever it was who had them. That person brought them up and she looked at them very slowly. All of a sudden, she took the whole bunch of pictures together, tore them up, and threw them in the wastepaper basket. All of us were standing with clenched fists. She says, "That's all, you can sit down." And that was it. You know, first humiliation, then destruction of property. You know, she could have put them in her desk and waited until afterwards, or a week or whatever, and then given them back.

Punished for Doing What I Had to Do

I was a junior in high school and this was the only time that I ever had to go to the principal's office. I was in an accelerated English class. One day, we had a substitute teacher and we were all supposed to work on our projects. The project that I was working on, while she just sat in the front of the room, required that I go to the library to look up some things. When I requested a pass to go to the library, she said "No." She told me that I had to stay in the room and that I couldn't leave. So, for some reason I decided that I had to give her an argument about how I couldn't do what I was supposed to do without going to the library. She wouldn't buy it. Eventually, I just ended up by saying, "Well, look, I'm supposed to finish this report and in order to finish it I have to go to the library. I'm going to the library." And then I left. And then what happened was that I got called into the principal's office. It wasn't all that serious. I think they made me stay after one day. But it was unjust. I got punished for doing what I had to do.

A Huge "F"

I was in second grade. We had weekly spelling tests and I had gotten 100 on all of them until one day in January. That day we had a substitute teacher. Since I was one of the tallest children in the class, I sat in the back of the room. We were doing the spelling tests. I never knew what I did that made her think I had cheated. But suddenly she came up behind me and with her red pencil wrote a huge "F" on my paper. I cried the rest of the day.

If I Didn't Know You, I Would Have Flunked You

When I was in junior high school, 1936 or 1937, I was really taken with the print shop. I learned how to set type, I could read it upside down and backwards, I could ink and operate the printing press. Name it and I could do it in the print shop. If I had my way, I would have been there all day every day, doing whatever it was that Mr. Connery, the shop teacher, needed to have done. And if he didn't need to have anything done, I wanted to be there anyhow. If nothing else I could straighten out the pieces of type in the type cases.

Of course, I still had to go to my classes, including gym 2 or 3 days a week. One day, and I can't remember just why, just before gym I went in to see the gym teacher (his name was

Tommy Green) and I said, "Mr. Green, can I be excused to go and work in the print shop?" He said, "Sure."

That was the start of a pattern that lasted about 8 weeks, the length of a marking period. That is, at the start of each gym class I would go to see Mr. Green and request permission to go to the print shop. It would be granted with no questions asked.

Came the day of reckoning at the end of the marking period. Report cards were given out and I found myself walking home with a D in physical education. My parents were not too impressed with the academic content of gym, so bringing home a D, my first and only, was not an experience I feared too much—but enough. Nevertheless, why the D? I had done nothing wrong.

The next day I took myself to Mr. Green's office and raised the question. And here is the reply from the teacher who had given me permission to cut gym and go to the printing shop. "Gee, if I didn't know you, I would have flunked you." And this after he had said it was OK.

Be Honest, Even If It Hurts—And It Did

I should say from the outset that I am fundamentally opposed to "nun-bashing" stories because I generally find them to be so one-sided. I was educated for 16 years in institutions run by nuns, and I would count my education as being somewhat above average. The nuns I have encountered, on the whole, have been dedicated, reasonable women, who were devoted to forming their students into well-rounded individuals. But I sure have a different memory about this one time.

She was my seventh-grade teacher, and she was also the principal of the building. I remember envying my friends who went to public school because they got to go to something called "junior high school." Somehow that seemed to be something interesting and really grown-up. I had to sit in the same room with the same teacher all day, while my friends got to change classes and have different teachers.

Most of us, with the worldly wise perspective of seventh graders, considered our teacher to be a little off her rocker. She was a strict disciplinarian and had a penchant for putting a bow on anything that stood still long enough—including the girls in her class. She was not a person to be trifled with, in spite of her quirky habits, so any rebellion we harbored did not usually express itself in open defiance. We saved it for the schoolyard and the bus home.

This is not to say that we were perfect angels. There was a fairly normal amount of talking out of turn, even though it was severely frowned upon. This tendency, plus my literal interpretation of the commandments I was studying, was what got me into trouble with Sister Jane.

Though catechism, or the study of church doctrine, was always part of the curriculum, it was intensified during the seventh-grade year since we were preparing for our Confirmation. We were all studying hard because we knew that the bishop was coming and he could ask any one of us a question to test our knowledge.

Naturally, "Thou shalt not bear false witness against thy neighbor" figured prominently in the discussion of the commandments at the heart of the catechism. We were lectured at length about the evils of lying and the terrible things that might result. No one saw fit to tell us about the fixes we could find ourselves in if we told the truth.

I was generally a "goody two-shoes" in school and fairly inclined to do as I was told. I did have two good friends sitting on either side of me, however, so temptation was always there. Cathy and Carrie were also great friends so they would frequently talk across me while I leaned back to give them room. I was caught in this collusion one day as Sister Jane fixed me with her eagle eye and said, "There's Miss Carter on the one side, and Miss Eckland on the other side, and Miss Lubal in the middle ready to be devoured."

There were snickers from the rest of the class, more directed at the teacher's inventive use of imagery and delivery than at me, I suspect. Still, with all the self-consciousness of a seventh grader, I took it very much to heart.

I felt somewhat miffed at being held up as the object of ridicule when I hadn't done anything wrong. When she called out my name a few minutes later, therefore, I mumbled, "That's my name, don't wear it out," under my breath in secret defiance.

Well, obviously, it wasn't secret enough because she could tell I had said something that she hadn't heard. She summoned me to the front, demanding to know what I had said.

It was a long and very public walk to the front of the room. I was scared because I knew that I had committed a no-no but it never occurred to me to make up a convincing lie.

When I got there she said, "I want to know what you said." She seemed to tower over me though she couldn't have been more than a few inches taller than I was. I said in a subdued, though courageous voice (after all, I had truth on my side), "That's my name, don't wear it out."

I don't remember the expression on her face because I was too preoccupied with her hand coming at me. She placed her hand on my face with her palm pressing on my nose. It wasn't brutal or physically abusive; it was more surprising than anything else.

"I'm going to push your face in, you bold article!" she said in an outraged voice. "I'm going to push your face in!"

I don't clearly recall what happened after that. I imagine that I probably looked as though I were about to cry, because there were no further repercussions from the incident, as I remember. I didn't have to write something a hundred times or do an extra page of arithmetic problems, which were the normal punishments for insubordination. The only thing I was left with was a sense of moral indignation that I had told the truth, as I had been instructed to do, and it hadn't saved me from getting into trouble. And I also learned that truth and self-interest aren't always compatible.

I Stepped on His Lunch

This was in the third grade. I was coming to school with the other kids and we went in the side door. We went through a cloakroom area, and it was very dark and you couldn't see, especially if you were outside and it was snowing (as it was). My eyes were becoming acclimated to the light as I walked through. There were probably 75 kids in the room that was actually a part of a furnace room. They had just put shelves in there where we would put our boots and lunches, or whatever.

I had a teacher that year who was known as the meanest in the entire school. Everyone hated her. Anyway, it was my misfortune that as I stepped through the door in my overshoes and my big, heavy winter coat, carrying my books and my lunch, I stepped squarely on some other kid's lunch as the kid was trying to put his boots and books away. The teacher grabbed me by the nape of the neck, shook me around in my coat, yelled and screamed at me, told me that I was a terrible person and that good people didn't step on other people's lunch. Then she proceeded to take my lunch away from me and gave it to the kid whose lunch I had stepped on and gave me his lunch, saying that that was what I was going to eat for the day.

It was really an unjust experience and I'll remember it forever. What I remember and why I remember that experience is the feeling of total helplessness against a person in a position of authority. I really felt in that situation that I was a thing and not a person.

Don't Disobey the Rules, for Any Reason

One morning in the third grade, my teacher (older, extremely strict to the point of being mean and unfair) listed about eight assignments on the board, gave instructions on how to complete each, and passed out many dittos to go with them. She then told us to remain silent and seated. No one for any reason was about to disobey her rules.

She left the room at that point and all was silent. Even the "bad" children were afraid to act up. After a while, another third-grade teacher (young, new to the building) poked her head in our door and asked, "Where is Mildred? . . . I mean Mrs. Carroll?"

Nobody would answer her because they were afraid, but I couldn't hold back any longer. I said, "I don't know. She is either on the phone or on her coffee break because she has been gone for 20 minutes, and she loaded us up with seat work to keep us busy before she left!"

Well, I think Mrs. Carroll got into a lot of trouble because when she came back to the room she was irate. She made me put my desk in the front of the room and began to lecture the entire class about rudeness and being inconsiderate. She then hit me over the head with her "pointer" stick. I had big tears forming in my eyes. At lunch, she made me sit between two boys and told me to keep my *mouth shut*. She also said if I went home and told my parents that I would be in even worse trouble!

That was the end of the incident but it left a bitterness in my mind and I still can remember how unfair she was to me.

Be Candid, But Watch Out

There was one incident I remember in the sixth grade. We were about ready to graduate. We had an art teacher whom none of us liked at all. We thought that the things that she did were ridiculous. She was a rather large woman and the boys in the class really kind of dumped on her. We would run around in the classroom and give her a hard time.

It was a warm sunny day, the day before graduation, and she asked us to do this assignment. She sat us down in the classroom. I still remember she was perspiring quite profusely and we wanted to get out of there. She said, "Now I want everybody to take out a paper and pencil and write to me very sincerely about your feelings about my art course." And she passed out the paper. It was yellow paper with blue lines. We had our own pencil. We didn't have ballpoint pens. She sat back down at the desk and I can remember the boys looking around the classroom and saying, "Now, we've got our chance. Now we've got her this time." She stressed that we had to be candid about our experience. "I really want to know what you thought of my art course." So we really kind of laid it onto her.

There were three or four of us who let her have it—all ways. We thought it was boring, that the things that she asked us to do were of no interest, and on and on and on. She gave us about 20 minutes to do it. The crew that I hung around with finished probably in around 10 minutes. We managed to pass our papers around and got to giggling. And the time was up and the other teacher came into the room.

Well, the next morning before graduation exercises, we were called down to the principal's office and soundly chewed out for having written such embarrassing things about this teacher. We were threatened by not being allowed to go to the graduation ceremony unless we, as a group, went to this teacher and apologized to her. We marched to the art room, which was down in the cellar. I can remember the cold cement wall downstairs, and we were a little nervous because our families were all ready for the ceremony. We really weren't sure what the upshot was going to be, but we went down and we talked with her. Her cheeks were red and she was still upset to think that we wrote something like that. We more or less hung our faces down and looked at the ground and apologized to her and we were allowed to graduate. But I'll always remember the two-facedness of that woman. We were told to be honest and then punished for it.

And I Had to Apologize

It was in the first grade. My teacher's name was Miss Street. She had white hair with a bun in back. It must have been the first week of school or shortly thereafter, and I still remember it to this day. My seat was toward the back, but not in the last seat. And behind me was this huge first grader. He was one of these very large, fat kids but so tall and heavy that the kids called him "Fat Franky." The teacher was handing something out and was giving directions. I was sitting in front of Franky and he didn't understand something and he asked a question. I turned around and clarified the directions for him and the teacher said, "Are you talking? You're not allowed to talk," or something to that effect. And something happened again and Freddy was confused and again I clarified for him. "You're talking again," the teacher said to me. "The next time you talk you'll be in big trouble," or something like that.

This is in a short span of time. It was in the afternoon and I must have talked again and she said, "All right, this is the third time. You've been talking too much," and she took a terry cloth towel, and she gagged me.

This humiliated me. Tears welled in my eyes and I eventually worked this thing loose. She saw it and she said, "You took that off your mouth." It didn't matter that I was choking on the damned thing. She said, "All right, I don't want you in my class any more. I don't want you as a student in my class. Leave this room and go to Miss Netty's class and tell her that you're to be a member of her class. GET OUT!" And I got up and walked out in the hall. The rooms opened off this center hall. I stood there. I was 5 years old at the time and I thought, "There ain't no way that I'm going in that room," and I went out the front door.

It must have been about two o'clock and I knew then that if I went home at that time it would raise all kinds of questions. So instead, I just wandered around and I finally found this kid who wasn't old enough to go to school. He was in his yard, and he said, "Oh, did you come to play with me?" and I said, "Yes." And I played with him until about 3:15 or 3:30 and then I headed on home, and when I got home my mother was frantic. She said, "Where have you been?" The police had been by, and so on, and so on. What had happened was, of course, that the teacher came out to check on me and went into the room next door and there was no kid.

So, somehow the message was that I had to go the next day and apologize to her for creating such a problem. All would be well if I apologized. So I got up earlier than usual and went and waited until I saw the teachers coming in before the kids. I went and told her that I was sorry for what I did. She said, "Oh, I hope so and I hope it never happens again." But we got to understand one another and that was the end of the incident.

I remembered that incident when I became a teacher. I had this new kid. I remember his name. It was Bobby Binton and after 2 weeks he still hadn't acclimated. He was being difficult. I said, "Bobby, step outside a minute," because I didn't want to bawl him out in front of the class and I said to myself, "This kid is going to take off." He was doing what I did. And that happened a couple of times and I went right after him and sure enough he was taking off. "I don't like this class," he said.

Get Here On Time

One situation stands out in my mind. It happened when I was in the eighth grade.

All young women were required to take home economics in that grade. The program consisted of one semester of cooking and one semester of sewing. The first semester I was assigned to cooking class, which I enjoyed very much. The second semester I had sewing. The sewing room was on the third floor of the school. The period before I had gym way down in the basement. I had had no problem at all first semester getting to cooking class on time. Thus I did not anticipate that second semester would be any different.

Indeed, I was able to get to the sewing classroom each day on time. The first few weeks we learned the basics. Soon we were ready for our first project. We got patterns for blouses, cut them out, and basted the parts together. So far so good! I was feeling very confident that I would receive a good grade in the class because I had gotten over 90% on all of the written examinations, as well as on the cutting and basting of the pattern.

The teacher demonstrated how to use the sewing machines. We all took turns practicing. Then she said that, because there were not enough machines for each student, those who arrived first would have first chance at them. The rest of us would have to wait. And under no circumstances were we to work on the projects at home. They must remain in the classroom at all times. She also said that we must meet the deadlines she had set for the completion of the project, or we would fail for the quarter.

I wasn't too worried at first, but as the weeks went by, it became clear that I was never going to be one of the first ones in the classroom. It was just too far from the gym to the third floor. The other girls all seemed to get a chance to use the machines. Each would sew her blouse, take it to the teacher, and either be told to continue or to rip out the seam and start again.

I was getting more and more nervous about my project, so I stayed after class one day and asked the teacher what she could suggest I could do about my problem. She answered, "Get here on time to get a machine." I explained that I didn't think that was ever going to be possible.

"May I come in during my study hall or after school?" I asked.

She said, "No." There would be no machine available during my study hall period and she wasn't going to stay after school with me.

I certainly didn't want to fail the quarter, so I decided to take the project home and complete it. Each day I would take the blouse home and spend about a half an hour using my mother's sewing machine. The next day I would ask the teacher to check my work. She always did, sometimes accepting the work, sometimes requiring that I do it over. But, she never asked me how I was getting the sewing done.

I got a good grade on the project, but I always felt guilty that I had disobeyed the teacher's instructions. I also felt angry that, even though I asked for help, I had to solve the problem myself.

I Still Vow My Innocence

I was in my kindergarten class and the teacher singled me out and one other girl from the class as the ones who crayoned on the floor. Although to this day I still vow my innocence, I was punished. We were taken into the hall and hit with a ruler.

I Have Never Forgotten the Pain

In the fourth grade, we had a student teacher, and the "real" teacher went out into the hall to allow this student teacher to take over. Apparently she did a terrible job, and the teacher in the hall came back and asked, "Who was talking?" because she had heard a terrible disruption in the class. Nobody raised his or her hand except me. I raised my hand and she said, "Eleanor, you are staying after school for talking." I knew that everybody had been talking but I didn't say anything because I was told never to tell on my friends. So I stayed after school at lunch time. This was especially difficult because my friends on my street all waited for me for lunch and she made me stay.

I had to write a letter to her apologizing for talking in front of this student teacher. I wrote the letter in my very best hand-writing and I didn't realize it but I had spelled *sincerely* wrong. I went up to her three times. Three times she looked at the letter and she said, "Look at it again. There is something wrong." I then told her, "Four of my friends are waiting for me to go home for lunch and they can't go home for lunch unless I am with them." So she allowed me to go home for lunch.

When I came back to the school, after lunch, she made me go through the same process. And I wrote the letter another time. Finally, the poor old lady said, "Eleanor, you have not spelled *sincerely* correctly." And I went to the dictionary, looked up sincerely, and spelled it correctly.

Then she thought she would take care of the whole experience by allowing me to lead the spelling test in the afternoon. I remember giving the spelling test, thinking that this is totally unfair and that I had no way to go up to her and explain to her the fact that she was unfair to me. I never forgot the situation and to this day, as a teacher, I listen to stories over and over again because of that experience. I have never forgotten the pain. I have never forgotten the four kids waiting for me to go home for lunch.

I Didn't Do It

This is a story about my gym teacher. One day, he took our class out to a little park where I think we had been doing some jogging and stuff. I remember sitting down and he was going to lecture us about something or another. Somebody made a sarcastic remark about what he was saying and he accused me of having said it. It was somebody near me but it was not I. I said, "I didn't say that," and he said, "Yes, you did." I said, "I didn't say it," and he said, "Yes, you did and I want you to get up and run 500 yards down around the tree and back." And I said, "Well, I didn't do it," and he said, "Yes, you did." So it came down to that sort of confrontation in front of the class. He was a vindictive type. So I got up and ran and I got to the tree and I said, "That's it, I'm not going back." But I turned around, and I did go back but stayed on the edge of the class and just left as soon as possible.

I Did Not Ask for Your Story

This incident is about me and a junior high school principal. I was in seventh grade. I was an average student. I went to classes and stayed with my group of friends.

One day in English class, two boys, Jim and Eric, started to tease another boy, Georgie. They were saying things that would understandably upset a seventh grader, things such as "Georgie takes ballet lessons and wears a tutu."

Georgie got tired of being teased and decided to go to the principal about it. The problem was that Georgie was afraid of Jim and Eric and thought that if he told on them that they would beat him up. Jim and Eric were friends of mine so Georgie told the principal that it was I who was picking on him.

I was called out of class and down to the principal's office. I had no idea what was going on. As I stood in front of the principal's desk, he yelled at me for teasing someone who never bothered me and told me what a mean youngster I was. When the principal was done, I began to tell my side of the story. I managed to get three words out and the principal looked down at me and said, "I did not ask for your story. Whatever you say doesn't matter. I know that Georgie wouldn't lie so just be quiet until I'm through." I began to cry and the principal told me not to be a baby. Georgie just sat on a chair in the office and smiled. The principal looked at me once again and said, "You have 2 weeks detention and I better not hear about you causing any more trouble. Go back to class." I walked out of his office, crushed.

Peer Relationships: Powerful Social Highs and Lows

Recently, one of us (Arthur) came across a picture of his sixth-grade class at the Roger Sherman School in New Haven, Connecticut. There we were, about 30 of us, sitting on the front steps of the school as our picture was taken. The year was 1933, 60 years ago as this is being written. Oddly enough, he was able to recall the names of about one third of that class and the faces of many more. And although there are no sharp memories of any event associated with these classmates (except for a clear recollection of Henry Welton living on Winthrop Avenue), the fact that the memory of the names is still alive speaks to the importance of these people in the early school years. And that is what this chapter is about—memories concerning one's fellows in school.

Put another way, the point is this: If the relationships that had any meaning in schools were only those between teachers and pupils, the experience of going to school and staying there for 12 or 13 years would be a much less complicated affair than it is. Like it or not, however, other kids are there and for numbers of people it seems their most vivid memories focus on something that happened with a peer or a group of peers. It is almost as though, as we learn from many of these narrations, the only thing that mattered in school was the friendship, or sometimes the nonfriendship, of other kids.

This last point can be understood as a possible function of several things: boredom and thus a concern with one's peers in order to escape it; inadequate academic performance and thus an effort to receive ego enhancement in other areas of one's life; in many cases, just plain adolescence; or the need simply to be accepted as a valued, or at least not a devalued, member of one's peer group.

Regardless of the source of the memories about one's school-mates, the fact is that many of the experiences of being called names, of being teased, of conspiring or competing, of playing pranks, of being rejected, and so forth, find their way into our permanent recall system. For the most part, these are powerful memories, we think, and they speak to a side of school that frequently gets simply taken for granted. To take that side of school life as a given, not worth much thought, may be a mistake, as a careful reading of the anecdotes in this chapter will indicate.

There is, of course, another thought that attaches to our concern here. It is that, much as a youngster's experience with teachers and other adults in school starts to provide lessons about how to deal with authority figures in the world outside the family, so do experiences with other youngsters start to provide lessons about how to deal with peers in that same world. In a world where maintenance of the group through intimacy and nurturance is not the norm, we do not think it is overly dramatic to suggest that peer life in school is one of the social crucibles through which a young person begins to learn what the interpersonal and group world is all about and how to best make his or her way in it.

As the reader will discover, most of the memories retained by our respondents were unhappy ones. Kids, indeed, can be ruthlessly mean to other kids. As will become clear, the root of the meanness is usually some kind of apparent deviance—physical, behavioral, socioeconomic, or what have you. In any event, it is evident that the unwritten curriculum provides the opportunity for learning some very powerful social relations lessons.

Always Being the Last Picked

You must understand that my vivid memory of school is colored by the fact I contracted polio when I was five. So you can imagine some of my problems.

I hated school, and my only memories and first thoughts of school both in grammar school and up until my junior year in high school were very unhappy ones. I can recall doing anything I could so as not to bring the other kids' attention to the fact that I was different than they were. One of my favorite tricks for getting myself in the front door of the school was to walk slowly until I spotted another student about to go in. Then I would hurry up behind them so that no one else would see me struggle with the door. Here's another thing. A practice in many classrooms is for the teacher to appoint two kids who would then take turns picking other kids to form a group or team. In order to avoid the embarrassment of always being the last child picked, I would go into the bathroom and wait an appropriate amount of time and then come out. As I was the last one left, the teacher would tell me which group to be in.

I can remember the other kids picking on me and making fun of the way that I walked. The strange thing is, I could not see myself walking as they depicted me. My mental image of myself was just like any of the other kids in school.

If I had to say only a few things about what I remember about school, I would have to say that I remember with such vividness that hurt that I felt. It was one of the most unhappy times of my life. I am not sure what happened, but in my junior year in high school things started to change and I began to enjoy school a bit better. It never was what other kids seemed to be experiencing, but it was an improvement over earlier years.

The Cost of Being One of the Guys

I was in high school and I was involved in shop. I grew up on a farm so that was fairly natural to me and I enjoyed it a great deal. I had a solid A, and not only that but the shop teacher had sort of gotten to be more and more a friend of mine. It turned out that one of his sisters, back in Cedar Falls, was a close friend of my cousin and I knew his sister. There were all kinds of linkages that made me very special to him. That in itself would have been fine except that he started more and more to single me out for favored treatment. I started to get heat from the other students about, "What's going on here? What kind of a teacher's pet are you? What are you doing?"

I didn't encourage him. In fact, I got so I would avoid contact with the guy. It was really too bad because he helped me out with my interest in architecture. He set me up in a class to make model houses and communities in order to encourage me towards an architectural career. At that point in time it was just great. I was well on my way. I loved math, drafting, and all of the things that would go with architecture. I was really moving in that direction. But one day his attention to me just got to be too much, and I set up a situation where I deliberately humiliated him in front of the whole class. I can't remember exactly what I said or did, but it was very deliberate and it was done in such a way that I knew he would have to be very hurt, get very angry at me, and that he would destroy our relationship. And that would prove to the other kids that I wasn't seeking favors and it would stop *their closedness*. It did, but you know, I've often wondered since what it may have cost me; for sure, that was the end of me being an architect.

Treated Like I Was Important

The experience that really stands out in my mind is Field Day during fourth grade. I was in the softball-throwing contest. There were eight boys, one from each of the other fourth-grade classes and myself. We threw three balls each and the person who threw the furthest ball won. I actually threw the furthest ball! I had beaten all the other boys and was treated like I was important. That was the first time I had beaten anyone at anything besides a game of cards or Monopoly.

Hey, Boy!

It was the first day of third grade. I was wearing a white shirt and my favorite jeans. I was walking outside on my way to the classroom when I heard a group of boys. One of them yelled, "Hey, boy!" So I ignored them, because I was a girl and I knew they were trying to tease me. They then came running over and tripped me. I fell to the ground and began to cry; not because I was hurt physically, but because one of them then said, "He's not a he. He's a sissy girl that just looks like a boy." I knew I had a short haircut and wore jeans a lot, but I never thought someone would actually mistake me for a boy. I cried for the next week during recess everyday, because they continued to make fun of me. Finally, I told my teacher. She understood how hurt I was, and those boys were held in from recess for 3 days. After that, I vowed to myself never to have short hair again!

An Oval Face

I was in the second grade. The teacher said, "Everybody come up to the front table and pick out one of the two shapes of paper." She explained that the shape you pick was to be similar to the shape of your face, round or oval. Next thing I knew, all my friends went to the table and chose the round pieces of paper, while I stood by watching. It seemed as if I was the only girl in the world who chose the oval-shaped piece of paper. That certainly ruined my day. The reoccurring question for the next few weeks was, why was I so different from the others and why was my face so ugly?

All the Same People

I went to an advanced-standing high school. This was back in the late 50s. It was a very unusual social situation. There were a lot of fairly wealthy people in school, a lot of people with a lot of money. Even though my father was a General Motors executive at that time and we were doing OK, by that school's standards I was not very high up on the ladder. It was the tightest social situation that I have ever been in. I felt very awkward because there were these sororities and fraternities and I couldn't get in.

It was the same thing with the service organizations. All the same people who were in the right sororities were asked to serve in those nice little service organizations and were on student government.

It was kind of an unhappy time for me and I was very hostile toward the situation. Even though I turned out to have a 4.0 average and I was one of four valedictorians out of a class of 459, I never felt that good about the whole thing. This was also a time when it wasn't that great for a woman to be that smart. I even had some guys who would call me for my homework. I was a fish out of water.

I Was the Keep Away

This was in the eighth grade. I was a small person, much less than 5 feet tall. I had a bunch of friends who were also small and we banded together because we were always getting picked on. On nice days nobody ever spent much time in the cafeteria. We always went out to play using as much time as was available. One of the most popular games at lunch time was "Keep Away." Usually, a large bouncing ball that you might use in playing kickball is the object that people use for Keep Away. The game was pretty much organized by what elementary school you went to. That is, two elementary schools converged on this particular junior high school. That's how the teams were picked up. The games were usually pretty rough, and we small people usually didn't fare very well in them, especially if we had the object to be used for Keep Away.

Then, one day, one of the bullies on the other team got upset with one of my friends, not with me but a guy who had the ball and was not giving it up when he should have. He just said to a bunch of his larger friends, "Well, let's use Lincoln." And so two guys grabbed me off my feet. I guess they sort of carried me, one by my torso and one by my legs, and just started running around. And it was such a wonderful idea, I guess, that everybody got right into it instantly. It was like they all had known that this was the way to play Keep Away all their lives. They had always wanted to play with somebody. Nobody stood around and said, "What the hell's going on here?" They just all got right into racing around the playground with me, tossing me back and forth to one another on the same side. I was lucky that my clothes did not get ripped, that I didn't eat too much dirt, and that I was smart enough to not get mad because I had no alternative. After a while the novelty wore off. I don't remember what it was that made people finally put me down on the ground in the end. That was the last time I played Keep Away. I moved to softball after that.

We Didn't Feel Courageous

One of my most vivid memories of school concerns a boy named Michael. Michael had an excruciating problem: He urinated involuntarily in class. I remember sitting next to him for an entire year in sixth grade. Once a week or so, Michael would have an "accident," class would be stopped, and often he would have to clean up around his desk as well as change his pants.

In many ways, Michael was the sort of student teachers seemed to enjoy. He was quiet, polite, intelligent, and studious. But each successive teacher during grade school grew to dislike him. His "problem" was disruptive and each left the impression that she believed that if only he set his mind to stopping it, it would stop.

Not surprisingly, his classmates found Michael an attractive target for all kinds of jokes. He had a conspicuous weakness that was easy to make fun of and, when taunted, he got satisfyingly furious. They knew they could bother him. And they knew, too, that he was too small to threaten any of the boys (and sometimes girls) who led the kidding.

I forget now what started the incident, but one day all but a few of the 25 or so members of our class followed Michael home after school. They milled after him, teasing, chanting his name, and occasionally throwing stones at him. Before long, he began to run headlong, in tears, with several of the boys running behind poking him as he went.

Those of us who didn't participate in the abuse, but who also did nothing to stop it, felt an odd embarrassment. We were embarrassed because we didn't know how to behave. We could tell the teacher, but then we would be informers. Or we could stand up to the group, but we didn't feel courageous. This was one of the first times that I realized how weak I could feel in the face of hostility.

The First Naked Shower

The incident I remember is the first time that we had to take a shower in public. It was in the seventh grade, after school, and we had just come in from our first soccer practice. Nobody would strip because we were just growing our pubic hair. The coach came in and yelled at us. I can remember his name was Ed Small. And Ed said, "I want you guys to take a shower and you have 5 minutes," and he left. And nobody would pull down their pants first. He came back in 5 minutes and called us all together and yelled at us again. "Goddammit, I told you guys I want you to take a shower!" and just then we heard the water running in the shower, and in the shower was a kid named John Netting. We thought, "My God, if John can take a shower, we can," and we all went in and there was John, taking a shower in his gym shorts.

I Was Cutting in on Her Territory

This is a story about being moved from second to third grade. I guess it was during a period when people were worried about doing something like rapid advancement, or something like that. I was tested by the school principal whose name was Mary Baines. I was very impressed with her because she had a doctorate. She was very nice to me. She gave me one of those individual IQ tests and then decided that I was too bright and was doing too good work to be in second grade so that I should be moved into third grade.

What happened was when I went into this class there was one girl that was sort of class leader and she had a crush on this boy. Her name was Betty and his name was Jim, Jim Howard. And he thought I was cute, too, so he started being nice to me and Betty got mad at me because I was cutting in on her territory. So she got this other guy, Bob Hall, who later became a policeman, and Betty and Bob would chase me home from school every day at lunchtime. They followed me and if they caught me, they would beat me up and tell me that I had to stay away from Jim. If I was lucky, I got away quick and ran fast and got the whole way home. This went on for several weeks and it was really an uncomfortable situation. I was saved by the fact that my sister got scarlet fever and was quarantined and I couldn't go to school. I missed the last 6 weeks of school.

Battling the "System": Sometimes a Winner and Sometimes a Loser

Earlier we took note of the fact that for most youngsters going to school represented, among other things, their first experience in formal organizational life. It seems to be true that as pupils move through the lower grades and into junior and senior high school, the opportunities to learn the workings of the system, to learn how to survive its absurdities, to learn about its impersonalness, and to learn how, at times, to make it work for you increase. This is so for at least two reasons. First, students do indeed grow and become wiser and certainly may become less willing pawns of the system or the individuals in it. Second, schools beyond the elementary level are more complex as organizations, thus presenting students with a greater variety of bureaucratic situations with which they must learn to cope or become victimized by them. For example, they must learn how to live and cope with not only the macrosystem of the school itself but with the microsystem of the classroom of each teacher they are scheduled to visit on any particular school day.

Another way of thinking about a youngster's inevitable confrontation with the school as a social system is to suggest that this is where, over time, he or she begins to experience and understand the meaning of "organizational politics." That is, it becomes quickly evident, we think, even for the less-than-acutely-perceptive boy or girl, what one has to do to get along, what kind of things to say to whom, and what kind of things not to say. Powerful lessons are learned from all this, although no one sets out to teach them.

There is an additional point that needs to be made here, and this is, again, one that we mentioned earlier. It is that most of the stories that we include in this chapter somehow involve the question of the discrepancy in power between youngsters and adults in school. There seems not to be much question that control of school life, for most interests and purposes, must reside with adults. However, there is also room to raise the question of whether or not, at times, the balance in a particular school or classroom gets knocked out of kilter in favor of the adults.

Having said all this, we should also note that there are not a great number of memories of individual-system (large one or small one) interaction. It may be that the situation that evokes "system" learning is, for the most part, too subtle to make a vivid mark in our memory. In any event, we have several narratives in this chapter that make the point well. They deal with a pupil's attempt to circumvent the system—a teacher's personal one or that of the school—or the pupil's being victimized by it, or so his or her memory interprets the event. In this latter regard, we refer to the last story, "Fifth Grade, Slow Class—Sixth Grade, Fast Class." This was told to us by a professor who ended it with, "Probably my goal in life is to end standardized testing." Clearly, in this man's experience the system had its effect on him, and not in a subtle way.

Finally, it's important to point out that there are times when an individual emerges victorious in his or her battle with the bureaucracy or with individuals in it. We have a couple of examples. One involves a youngster who would not sit still for being unjustly accused of cutting school. And there is another in which a student "beat" the grading system outright when he moved from one state to another, through ignorance of a school principal. This person is himself a highly successful principal who in that role, we suspect, has beaten the system any number of times.

Gotcha

I wrote a note to the school, signing my mother's name, asking that I be excused at 10:00 a.m. on that day. I was excused but I did not know that the principal had saved other notes written by my mother and he compared the handwriting. He went down to the house (two blocks away) and was in the living room when I walked in. My mother told him that she did not know I had written any notes and did not expect me home from school. I cried the rest of the day.

A Shortcut

This was in the first grade and my teacher was Mrs. Wessel. I remember sitting at my place trying to figure out my math problems. Next to me, on the floor, was a friend of mine whose name was Charlie. He had already finished his problems and was given permission to play. While I was trying to do my work (which always took me longer than the others because I was not very good at math), Charlie teased me because I was not yet allowed to play.

I was working away, trying to finish, when I thought of a shortcut. I simply chose any number for the answer, not bothering to actually figure out what was correct. In a few minutes, I handed my paper in to the teacher and, with a smirk on my face, I sat on the floor with Charlie and proceeded to play. However, when Mrs. Wessel noticed my answers and realized I had not tried to answer them methodically, she told me to get back into my chair, erase my answers, and seriously figure out each math problem.

By this time it was arts and crafts period, and Mrs. Wessel went to her desk and taught the class how to make butterflies out of colored tissue, clothespin, and pipe cleaners. And I was stuck in my chair finishing my addition while the class was having fun putting together their homemade butterflies.

After I had finished my math, I reluctantly went to Mrs. Wessel's desk and handed in my paper. I don't remember exactly what she said, but she handed me the butterfly she had made to illustrate to the class and told me I could keep it. I think I still have it.

A Curious Justice

This is a sad story. I was in my senior year in high school. It was February or March and I can remember walking home in the snow. All of the SATs and the college acceptance letters had come back, and everybody knew where they were going the next year. This was a college prep high school in a university town and 95% of the students were going to college. We were running through the hoops to finish up the end of the year. The teachers knew it and the students knew it. School seemed very, very meaningless.

It was at that time in 1965 that the Selma march was being pushed. A friend of mine and myself figured that though we didn't know exactly what was going on there, it seemed more important to be there than to be at school. So we took off, with $10 between us. I left a note for my parents. I didn't tell them. They didn't find it for 3 days. But we took off and hitchhiked down South.

Eventually got down to Meridian, Mississippi. I was feeling guilty so I called my parents. They were very understanding and said, "All right. Do it and come on back."

At any rate, we participated in the march on Birmingham. After about 2 weeks, we were running low on money. My friend flew back because his parents sent him some money. I hitched back. I remember walking through a snowstorm in my town. I took a bus across town, walked up to the house. It was early morning and my parents were there and were very understanding about the whole situation.

I got my things together and went off to school. I went to art class, my first class of the day, and I remember seeing this memo from the principal that I and my friend were to receive Fs for every day that we were gone. It was an unexcused absence. We were not to be allowed to make up any examinations and there would be no recourse. The art teacher showed it to me.

So here you have a major political and social event going on in which we took part. We came back to a high school where what was going on, from this principal's perception, was meaningful education. But from everybody else's perception, including the teachers, it was meaningless. And we were penalized for having this type of an experience. It was a curious justice.

Teacher Can Be Wrong, Too

It all began upon my first day of high school. As a freshman we were presented with restrictions that were not applicable to the upperclassmen. One of the rules that freshman had to follow was that we had to attend assigned study halls during our free periods. Meanwhile, the upperclassmen could leave the campus and go to McDonald's or Burger King.

As time went by, more and more freshmen began skipping their study halls and leaving the school grounds with the older kids. But I always went to the study halls because I was in fear of this one particular teacher. I figured, with my luck, if I skipped I would get caught anyway.

After the first month of attending these study halls, which in my mind was a waster because I never could do any work in them, the study hall teacher's attitude really began to bother me. So I started to consider skipping the class. "Why not?" I thought to myself, everyone else is skipping and no one seems to be getting in much trouble, although people were being threatened with suspension. But, of course, I never thought that would happen to me.

The next day, before the teacher came in, my friend and I were debating in our study hall whether or not we should stay or skip out. We both decided to leave, so we went outside to talk. Feeling a little guilty, we started debating whether or not we should just go back in. Just as we were debating about going back in, we saw the teacher leave the room, not realizing that he also saw us outside. We figured that if we went back in the room we would get there before he returned and maybe he would just think that we were late.

Well, to our surprise there was another teacher sitting in the room proctoring the study hall, so we just walked in and gave her our names. The teacher who was usually there never came back, but we thought nothing of it. Little did we know that our original teacher who always proctored left because he went down to the principal's office to turn our names in.

Later that day when I went home, my mother told me that she received a phone call saying that I had skipped study hall and as a result I was suspended. At first I could not understand how that could happen since I really did go to study hall, but then I realized that my original proctor must have seen us outside and did not know that we went into class late. Therefore, he must have assumed that we skipped and turned in our names. After explaining all this to my mother, she then proceeded to call the school and explain to them what I had just told her. The teacher was very stubborn and accused me of lying and said that he saw me outside and that there was no way I went to study hall. My mother, now getting angry with him, told him to go check with the other teacher who was proctoring after he left. But he refused, insisting that I skipped and now I would have to pay for it by being suspended. My mother realized that this conversation was going nowhere so she hung up with him and called the principal. The principal of my school was a really nice guy and he told my mother he would go and investigate the whole situation and find out the truth behind it. About 30 minutes later, the principal called back and said the teacher he had to talk with had left the school and so he would not be able to check this situation out until the next day sometime when he was through with his meetings that were scheduled. Therefore, I was unable to go to school that day. On the following day, I received a phone call in which the principal apologized for putting me through any inconvenience. The suspension was a mistake and it would not go on my record. He said it was a "terrible misunderstanding" and again he was very sorry.

As a result of this mishap, I got a free day off from school, and I proved my stubborn proctor wrong. However, it did bother me that he got the principal to apologize for him and that he could not do it himself.

We Still Chuckle About It

I was a sophomore in high school and I can remember having Mrs. Frete for English. I liked her as a teacher and as a person. She treated all of her students with respect and dignity.

She stressed writing in her class. She assigned a theme and a book report to be written each month. I enjoyed doing this. I was good at it and she was very generous with her praise. She would always write nice comments in the margins of your papers, noting how nicely you had turned a phrase or had constructed a paragraph that was key to the report.

I got sick during the second semester and didn't read a book in time for one of the required book reports. I was in a sad situation as the day for handing in the report approached. In a panic, I scanned the bookshelf in my sister's room for a book that could be read quickly and used for the basis of my monthly report. My eye fell on a masterpiece entitled, "Here Buster—The Story of a Seal." My sister Jill, an eighth grader, gave me her permission to sign out this work from her childhood collection, so that I might write my scholarly treatise.

I read the novel very quickly and prepared my report for submission even faster. After turning in my paper, several of my friends whom I had told of my plight began to warn me about Mrs. Frete. They said that her even demeanor was only a cover for her wicked temper that she used rarely, but with great vigor when a student tried to deceive her.

By the date that the book reports were to be returned, I was contemplating running away or throwing myself across her desk and asking for mercy. I would do anything that might save me from the torture that would surely be my fate.

When the papers were returned, mine had a C+ on it and a note to "see me" signed by Mrs. Frete. As class ended I waited meekly for her. She sat down at her desk and asked me if I was satisfied with my grade. I assured her that I was, indeed. She explained that she had given me a "C" for taking the initiative to read something—even though it was a third-grade level. She said she gave me the + for having the audacity to turn in the report. She asked me what I had selected for my next report, and I assured her it was a novel of which I thought she would approve.

She started to laugh and said that she never would have believed that any of her students would try to snow her with such a ridiculous book. She said that she laughed the entire time she had read my report, and that although she enjoyed the humor, I had better not try this again.

I assured her that I would not, and I left very pleased that some good had come of my masterpiece. To this day, my family and I have an occasional chuckle over my literary past.

Status Quoism

From the third grade to the ninth grade, I lived in California. I went to school in a very progressive school district. Then we moved back to Tennessee. In California I was in accelerated classes. I took algebra and French as a junior high student. When I went back to Tennessee, it was a very conservative school district and they asked me to sign up for what I thought I should take in tenth grade. Well, in tenth grade I should have been taking trigonometry, fourth-year French, and so on. I had had all the standard things so, very innocently, I put on my card that these were the things next on my program.

I was called into the office by the principal who proceeded to read the riot act to me. He had been the principal when my mother went to high school in that city. It was not yet integrated. It was resisting integration as hard as it could. He was going to make sure that nothing changed in his school, and he proceeded to tell me that I was no longer in California, that I was in the South, in a good, old southern high school that did things in a certain way. It was a horrendous experience. I was going to behave like everybody else in that high school and in 10th grade these were the things that you could take, and if I had had them before, it was just too bad. "This is what you take in 10th grade." And that's what I did. And also I decided that to survive in high school that I would be like everybody else. I could get my As without doing anything. But it was sort of a holding operation. I could not wait to get out of high school.

I Just Inflated My Grades

When I came to live in New York State in 1963, I had one set of transcripts that said A, B, C, and I had another set of transcripts that said 4, 3, 2, 1. The principal never having seen these said to me, "What is this?" So I conned him into believing we had different numerical equivalents in the school I came from. I took every grade to the maximum possible. A C became an 84 and a B became a 90, and so on. I just inflated my grades. I moved up in class standing that day faster than any kid in New York State ever did. I'm absolutely sure of that.

I Felt Like a Child All Over Again

I really remember the time I got caught leaving school grounds when I was in high school. This incident really affected me because I felt that I was treated unfairly and in a childlike manner.

It was my first week of my junior year. At the first grade meeting, we were told by our administrator about the rules and regulations to be enforced during that year. Of course, some rules remained the same from the previous year, others were slightly altered, while others were entirely new. The one rule that seemed to cause an uproar was the one concerning closed campus. Though our high school always had a closed campus, it was never enforced. Of course, my friends and I did not pay any attention to the rule and decided to go to McDonald's one day for lunch. We sneaked to the parking lot and left, not realizing that our administrator had followed us to the car. Sure enough, when we returned, he was waiting for us in our parking space.

What resulted from this incident was a day of suspension and 5 days detention after school. Obviously, this was a very harsh punishment. However, the administrator claimed that, since we were the first ones to break the rule, we should be the first ones to look like fools.

I felt like a child all over again. Here I was applying to colleges, working part-time, and paying for most of my expenses. I was finally starting to feel like an adult, yet the administrator took that feeling away. To him I was just another "kid" that deserved what I was getting. It was not the punishment that bothered me, it was the principle of the matter.

Fifth Grade, Slow Class—Sixth Grade, Fast Class

This experience started in the fourth grade. A group of us were members of the band and we would get excused for band practice. We had hour-long classes and band practice took up half of that hour. The teacher would become very upset when this happened. One day, we went to band practice and came back to find that the class was half an hour into an IQ test. We sat down and the teacher said, "You now have half an hour in order to complete the test." So we completed it along with the rest of the class. It was just another IQ test and we went on.

Afterwards, my parents got a call saying that I had a very low IQ. In fact, my IQ was so low and I had done so well in school that I was what we would call an exceptionally motivated child. I was an overachiever and the three other kids were labeled the same way. We were all considered overachievers.

The teacher continued this practice of giving tests when we were at band practice. Every time we went to band practice, she began conducting these classes in spelling, math, or social studies. At the very end of the year, each of us received three Fs in each of the respective areas as well as a very low IQ, which only further confirmed to my parents that I had a problem. I didn't know how to explain the situation. My parents were very upset and sent me to summer school to make up my work in social studies and math. The same thing happened with my three or four friends. The school wanted to keep us back. We did well enough in the summer school program, though, to be passed conditionally to fifth grade, but in the slowest group.

In the fifth grade we were given an IQ test again. This time the reverse happened. We were slow students, and because of this we were given more time than the other students, probably another hour. We popped out at the other end of scale and came up with another label. This time we were underachievers. And so one year, I was put in the very slow class in the fifth grade, and in sixth grade, the next year, I was put in a very fast class. And so, not until ninth grade, when I had a guidance counselor who went over my files, were they able to make any sense of what was going on. As I think about it, this changed my whole outlook on education. I don't believe in what I call this academic goal of education. I can't stand standardized testing. Probably my goal in life is to end standardized testing.

"Getting Even" by Playing
Tricks and Pranks

We have mentioned several times that schools, by organizational definition, are places where a few adults exercise a great deal of power over the activities and freedom of action of a large number of youngsters. Although this power is exercised most often with benign intent, there are also examples, as we have seen, when it is not.

In any system, the exercise of power by one group over another will at times provoke feelings of antagonism, if not downright hostility. The question is, What is to be done with these feelings? How does one "get even"? The answer, many times, is through humor and the telling of jokes among members of the less powerful group, the punch lines of which show off members of the more powerful group as stupid or engaging in acts that, quite appropriately, make them the butt of jokes.

We suspect that in some cases, particularly those that are related to organizational life, the humor gets translated into action through the playing of pranks. We think it may well be that schools are ideal places almost by design for one generation (the younger one, of course) to play pranks or to try to trick another. (The playing of pranks, as we shall see, can also be intragenerational.) The way schools are organized, the activities in which adults engage youngsters, and how they themselves engage in the activities are open invitations for students to try to make these same adults look silly or inadequate simply so they may be laughed at. This may sound cruel, and in a way it is, but we think it is also a statement of part of the reality of school life. In addition, it is probably no accident that the dreaming up and playing out of pranks seem to occur mostly in the junior or senior high school world and appears rarely to be part of elementary school life. Youngsters in the upper grades undoubtedly start to sense the meaning of independence that goes along with adolescence, and this sensing may well get acted out in behaviors designed to get even by making the "oppressor" look foolish.

Pranks are played with a sense of both hostility and affection. As will be seen, there are times when the object of the trick is to embarrass the other or to disrupt the other's life. There are other times when the object is purely to have fun. We also think that part of it has to do with discovering whether or not a particular adult can "take a joke." The playing of pranks on teachers may be a sort of psychological testing ground for adult-teenage relationships. And a fertile testing ground it is.

Although it is probable that teachers are the butt of most of the jokes that are played in school, other students come in for similar treatment at times. Sometimes the idea is simply to create a funny situation by exposing and making a particular behavior pattern seem ludicrous. Sometimes playing a prank, particularly if the perpetrators can remain secret, is a way of getting to a class bully who is, of course, an oppressor. "Up in the Insulation" is such an example and, on reading it, one has little trouble picturing the high glee of those involved.

A few words need to be said about the humor that will be evident in the narratives that follow. First, without much doubt what is seen as humorous is in the eye of the beholder. And what kind of "eye" any particular beholder has is a function of many things—one's age, work experience, marital status, how one spends one's days, and so on. Thus it will come as no surprise that a youngster's view of what is funny may well differ, and frequently does, from that of an adult. Interestingly, when adults talk about a child's having a good sense of humor, they often mean that the child sees humor in things in much the same way as the adult does.

We believe that there is a kind of humor that belongs, if not exclusively then almost so, to youngsters. Any moderately observant adult can see it in operation just by watching children at play for a while. Children simply find humor in things—and this goes for teenagers, too—that adults may understand but do not find particularly funny. And this, we suspect, is the way it should be.

So it is, then, that a number of the anecdotes we collected have to do with something that simply happened or was deliberately planned—a prank—that was viewed with high humor at the time but not so high on the retelling. The memories of that high humor, though quite evident, were tempered by comments like, "It doesn't seem funny now, but when it happened it was hilarious."

It Went Flat

In high school, this one kid would come in to algebra and he had a habit of throwing his books on his desk. One day, several boys in the classrooms got to his classroom earlier and took every screw out of the desk. The teacher came in and all the kids came in. Now all the kids were aware what had happened because these things get around. This kid comes in and just like normal he throws the books onto the desk and the desk went completely flat. Well, you can imagine how funny that was. The kid got into trouble, but not the kids that took all the screws out. Every time I see somebody throwing books around, I think about the kid that came in, threw his books on the desk, and the thing went flat. You just had to be there to see it.

We Were Going to Trick Her Back

My seventh-grade science teacher was one of my favorite teachers. Maybe it was because she was very animated, knew her stuff, made it interesting to the student, and had a good sense of humor. She tried to make examples or express a point in science by doing something that would bring it to mind well. One of the things that she did that became well-known—she did it class after class, year after year—was to make a point that two things can't be in the same place at the same time. And what she would do when she was giving this little lecture about that fact was that she would walk slowly up the aisle and then, suddenly, with some unsuspecting student, sit down in his chair and shove him out the other end of the chair and onto the floor. Then she would announce, "See, two things can't be in the same place at the same time."

Well, in our class, a couple of us decided that if she did that to us we would be ready for her. You see, she had a reputation for doing that, as well as other tricks. This happened to be the one that she was well-known for and one that we were going to use to trick her back. So, as she was walking down the aisle giving this lecture she started to sit down and shove one of my friends out of the seat. Well, he quickly got up, moved out the other side, and she sat down and almost ended up on the floor herself. The class laughed and she laughed and the point was still made. What was real important was that she had the kind of sense of humor that she could go along with the joke.

Break the Ruler

Belle Raine was our junior high math teacher and she always wore black. So we called her Black Belle. And if you ever misbehaved or even looked like you were going to, you had to go up in the front of the room, hold your hands up, palm up, and she'd swat you with the ruler. And if you ever pulled your hands away because you didn't want to get hit, then you had to put them out there and get hit twice. And the real goal was to see if we could get her to break the ruler while she was coming down. Every once in a while she did just that. We loved to watch her get mad.

Right Up to the Ceiling

We had a real mean and vindictive elementary teacher. So one night before Halloween evening, we must have had about 20 kids and for about a four-block radius we collected every porch swing, every garbage can, every chair, every table—anything possible—and completely filled up the front and back porch of her house, right up to the ceiling.

No More Erasers

I was a junior in high school and I was involved as a volunteer in the Audiovisual (AV) Department. A bunch of us met one afternoon and we decided it might be fun to take all the blackboard erasers in the building. The AV guys had master keys to get into all the classrooms, which we did. We took all the blackboard erasers, put them in a box, and we mailed them to the principal, but not before the next morning. It was sort of fun to watch the teachers respond to not having blackboard erasers and the responses of the few who had their erasers in their desks and the glee with which they exhibited them to the other teachers who didn't have any. It was a prank. It was one of those kind of Halloween nerdy respectable pranks that the guys who were the upstanding citizens of the school decided to pull.

Nothing ever happened, although I suspect the principal knew it was the AV guys, as they were the only ones who could have had access to those rooms. It was fun to watch the frustration of the teachers.

H'mmmm

My most memorable incident occurred on the day that the teacher hung up a poster with a picture of a radio. The lesson of the week obviously had something to do with listening to the radio. All of a sudden, the entire class started to hum. The humming continued until I got up, went over to the radio poster, and pretended to turn it off. The class was quiet until another student got up and pretended to turn the radio back on. We started humming again. This went on for about 10 minutes.

Up in the Insulation

I was no angel in high school. I joined the Radio and Weather Club, not because I was interested in meteorology or anything like that. It was because when you joined that club you had keys to all the closets in the school. Well, one closet led to the insulation of the high school and the other one led to the roof of the high school. And for a high school kid that was great. It meant all kinds of freedom.

I used to skip my last period of the day (study hall) and go to the Radio and Weather Club. We would climb up on the roof. And there was this little vent or draft with a cover. We'd lift that up and crawl in, and we were in the insulation but in the top of the auditorium where study hall was.

One day, we discovered there was a little window right below through which we could see the people studying. I don't know why we did this. We had no logic. We were just balancing on beams and if we fell either way we'd crash through the ceiling, but you don't think of that in high school. Right below was one of the most hated kids in the class, Bill Engles. We used to call him Uncle Billy. The only word he knew was f———. F——— this and f——— that, everything—f——— this and f——— that. And he was a bully. He beat up practically everybody when we were growing up and he was right below and within shooting distance. We couldn't resist. We had these pebbles that we had picked up on the roof. We started winging them at him and hitting him. The instructors were terrified. He was a big muscular boy. We did this for a few minutes and all of a sudden he stood up and said, "If you don't f——— stop

that f——— stuff, I'm going to knock your f——— head, whoever is f——— doing it." They didn't want to mess with him.
The guy said something like "OK, let's cool down. Whatever is
going on, let's knock it off." We couldn't knock it off. He didn't
know who did it. He thought it was someone in there. He
didn't know it was up on the roof. We just doubled our throwing. He finally stood up and said, "F——— you," and he just
walked out and no one dared stop him. And that was a happy
moment.

The Game Was That He Would Never Know

When I was about 13, I went to a private boys' school. We
had one teacher whose name was Borton. He was primarily an
English teacher. We had a nickname for every one of our teachers. Borton's nickname was Hosie. I don't know why but it was
Hosie. My feeling about my school in those days was that the
teachers were never in charge of the classroom, the students
were. Some teachers could deal with that better than others.
Some of them became very forceful and others simply over-
looked it. Hosie was one of the guys who chose to overlook the
fact that in reality the students were in charge of the classroom.
He was merely some kind of a figure at the front who occasionally wrote on the blackboard. He would get into reading Shakespeare for an hour or an hour and a half in English class. He'd
never take his eyes up from the book and he'd get caught up
totally in this Shakespearean drama, or whatever it was he was
reading. He would take all of the parts and act them out, mostly
to himself. And so in the springtime, the person sitting in the
back of the room next to the window would raise the window.
During the course of the class while Hosie Borton was reading
Shakespeare, taking all these different parts, one by one we
would disappear out the window. And the game was that he
would never know. And that we would have to get out of the
classroom and back in without him knowing it before he finished the end of the story. And we always were successful.

Learning About Learning and Other Valuable Lessons

A case can be made, of course, that everything a youngster experiences in school ultimately involves some type of learning. Nevertheless, the type or types of learning that may have resulted from the experiences recounted in previous chapters are not those usually associated with what going to school is all about. That is, they seem to be incidental to having been a pupil. However, we hasten to add that those experiences can be labeled as "unavoidable" and, in addition, they certainly were not unimportant. The reader may recall, for example, how some of the lessons about having been nurtured or embarrassed were very profound ones. It does indeed seem to be true that some very important things learned in school are then deposited in a youngster's "vivid-memory bank" from which "withdrawals" are made only at special times.

We found a number of memories that had very much to do with "learning"—although only a few had to do with a recollection of a particular school subject. Further, the reader will discover, or perhaps rediscover, that the teacher was not always central to the memory. At times, kids teach other kids lessons, in one fashion or another.

The reader will also discover that there are a few memories of learning something that one might not expect to find. They have to do with learning about learning or learning about the importance of learning. For example, we were really struck, as perhaps the reader will be, by the memory of a first grader who remembers being aware, for the first time, of thinking and of thinking about thinking.

There are a couple of other points that develop from these memories of learning "something." First, it was our impression that although our memory providers were quite spontaneous in their recounting of a learning event, it seemed to us that a good bit of prior reflection on the event had been involved. What this suggests is that the narratives presented in this section reflect a more intellectual approach to the situations they describe than has been the case in prior chapters. In many cases, it appears that the person has already engaged in an analysis of some experience in school that was concerned with their learning something—but a "something," as we pointed out earlier, that was, for the most part, not concerned with subject matter. What was remembered had a different quality than learning the formula for finding the area of a circle, for example.

Second, as will be readily apparent on reading, some type of experience qua experience was connected with every memory. In a curious way, it seems the vivid memories of learning something in school support the notion of an unwritten curriculum by communicating, in effect, the thought that what gets recalled about learning has some other triggering experience attached to it.

Finally, it should be noted that the stories about learning something in school only occasionally seem to carry the intensity of emotional impact that characterizes the majority of memories in the preceding chapters. Some of them, indeed, seem to carry little "zip" at all, although they seemed to be very close to the surface of the raconteur's memory. It may be that the type of emotion associated with these recollections is simply one that is harder for us to understand or to identify with. In any event, read on and make your own interpretation.

A Really Good Experience

I remember my seventh-grade art class. The teacher told us that we would be making a movie and that we had to fulfill every role in the making of a movie, from the writing of it, to the acting of it, to the filming of it. I recall that one of the girls in the class wrote it. She came in with a manuscript and there were various parts which we could try out for. But first, the teacher had to find out if we had acting ability, so he brought us in to the main office and into a guidance counselor's little office. It really was a cubicle. He brought in only one of us at a time and he asked us to imitate a person shaving himself. He sat opposite us. Well, at the time I sure didn't have any beard and really hadn't thought about even what it looked like to shave, other than to have watched my father in the morning. I tried to look like I was shaving but obviously was a flop at it, because he announced that I would not be one of the people acting in this film.

At the next class, we had the opportunity to try out to be a member of the "technical crew," and so I decided that I would try out for that. I had heard somebody say that the trick to being a good camera person is to move very, very slowly. You must never get flustered and jerk the camera. You had to be thinking ahead to know where you wanted the camera to be a few seconds later, so that you could be moving in that direction, moving in and out toward the action. And I recall standing on this teacher's desk with a small tripod camera and panning down to the simulated action he had created between a couple of students at a desk in the art room. And I remember heeding the directions I had heard and then subsequently being chosen to help film.

I remember every aspect of the development of that film. We had characters popping out behind a person who was walking down the hall. The way we did that was to first film the person walking down the hall and then put the film back in the camera, retake it of the head of a person against the black background and then retake it again with another person.

It was really a good experience. I do recall doing the title slides, bringing in music for it, and all of us getting together at the teacher's house, which was in the next town, one Friday afternoon and evening to look at all the footage and to talk about how we were going to edit it. I don't really know how long it took, whether it was a whole semester or whether it was four or five sessions. He was a model of a very good teacher for me.

A Bit of Humility

I was in the fifth grade. I was sitting next to this boy. I was kind of an intellectual snob and he really wasn't very smart. But one day I saw him drawing something that was really wonderful. I hadn't realized that he could do that and I knew that I couldn't do that. It really took me aback because it was my very first experience connected with school seeing somebody do something that I couldn't do. It stayed with me till this day. Kind of a bit of humility.

Untested Assumptions

One day, the phone in the classrooom rang, and after Sister Agnes hung up, she turned to the class, looked at me and said, "Sister Maria would like to see you in her office."

The classroom was on the third floor of a four-floor building. By the time I reached the main office, I was sobbing out of control. I couldn't imagine what I had done, but I knew I was in for it. When Sister Maria saw me, she exclaimed over my crying and wanted to know what was wrong. I managed to get out, "I don't know what I did, but whatever it was, I'm sorry. Please don't tell my mother and father."

She laughed as she responded, "You didn't do anything. I just needed a messenger to go over to Brother Patrick on the boy's side, and it was your class's turn to be called upon. You're not afraid of me, are you?"

What a ridiculous question. It took me an hour to calm down. But it resulted in a genuine perk for me; I soon became her "favorite" messenger, a role I loved to play to the hilt. But it took a lot longer for me to perceive a principal as anything less than fearsome.

Plagiarism Is Not Allowed

I was in the third grade. Mrs. Bolton was my teacher and she was really great. We had an assignment to make a science book on anything in science that interested us. I decided to make one on mineralogy. I had a mineral collection and I made a book on it with a beautiful hard cover. Choice specimens of minerals were glued into the book to illustrate the text. I also got some books from the library and I copied verbatim the descriptions of these minerals and the explanations of them. Mine was a beautiful-looking book and, as I think about it, its appearance seemed to be what was really important.

Well, I handed it in and a few days later the principal, Mr. Frankton, opened the classroom door and beckoned to me with his finger. He took me down to his office. Mrs. Bolton was there, too. He had my science book and really gave it to me about plagiarism, even though I didn't know what the word meant! He had some books from a local college library and showed me where what I had put into my science book came verbatim right out of those books, and this was not allowed. That lesson has stayed with me ever since, even though I'm not sure how to spell plagiarism. It's a "g," isn't it?

Territorial Prerogative—Prelude to Conflict

Fourth grade was a magic time. It was a time of being a good student and a very active, involved young lady. I was a Goody-Goody-Two-Shoes. I was teacher's pet. One day, the teacher asked me if I would do a certain task at recess time. It was something that I was pleased to do even if I had to stay in from recess. So I stayed in and started to work when one of my classmates walked into the room and decided he was going to help me. I would have none of that because I was the one who had been given the assignment and I was going to be the one to do it! He didn't agree and insisted on helping me. I kept telling him that he had no business there and that he should go out to recess where he belonged. He would not listen to me. So I took out my fountain pen, one of the vintage ones that would squirt. I said,"Billy, if you don't leave immediately I'm going to squirt you." He looked at me in disbelief and continued to harass me. I held the pen up and I squirted. And, oh my God, ink came out all over Billy's face. I think it's probably still on him. The teacher came in, scolded me, and made me stay in from recess for 2 weeks. I was no longer a teacher's pet. Mostly, I was shocked at myself that I could do something like that.

Watch What You Believe About Adults

I remember once when I was in third or fourth grade and my mother came to visit the school. Typically, the parents would visit from time to time but this was the first and the last time that my mother visited any class that I was involved in. It was kind of a "show-and-tell" event and all the kids were asked to get up and say something about something—whatever. It was my turn and I got up and I said something that I thought was noteworthy in that when my father was a small boy he used to eat worms. There was sort of an embarrassed silence and they pressed me on it. They said, "Are you kidding?" I said, "Oh, no, no, no, my father told me this and he wouldn't tell me anything that wasn't true." And then I got adamant and got very persistent. My mother seemed to get more and more agitated and I couldn't figure out why.

Anyway, what happened is that when Dad and I would walk around the farm he would sing songs and we would sing together and one of the songs he used to sing, "Nobody loves me, everybody hates me, guess I'll go eat worms." For him it was a song but for me as a third grader this was the truth. He was disclosing something about his own childhood, and I became quite incensed and angry that they weren't taking me seriously when I was passing on the truth. Looking back on it, I sometimes wonder how I could have been . . . so naive. It seemed crystal clear to me at the time.

Being Hoisted on One's Own Petard

When I was in junior high school, eighth grade, I found myself in an awkward position. I had been having a particularly hard time with my English teacher and we were not on the best of terms. It seemed that I could do nothing right or well enough for him, and I was faced with an upcoming report card grade that was less than I desired.

The last day of the marking period arrived and when I got to class, I discovered that I had forgotten that it was the day for our "in-class" book report. Not only had I forgotten that it was the day to write the report but I had forgotten to READ a book! So there I sat, an absolute mess, wondering if I should tell him or not. One more doghouse to put myself into. My heart started pounding and my palms got sweaty as my classmates took out their books and started to write.

After what seemed like hours (in reality about 3-5 minutes), I decided to cheat and just *invent* a book to do a report on. Knowing that it could be checked, I told my teacher that I had bought the book at a bookstore and had forgotten it at home, so I couldn't remember the name of the author, publisher, and so on. He was not happy. He told me that he would allow me to use it, but I would lose some points for not having all the necessary information.

Feeling more sure of myself, and figuring that a grown man would never want to find or read a teenage girl's novel, for the next 30 minutes I fabricated the most intricate teen romance story I could conjure up. I finished on time with an "analysis of the worth of the book" as instructed.

Three days later, I received my book report back with an A on it, as well as the words: "Sounds like a GREAT story for girls to read. Your analysis on its worth is excellent. Please let me know where I can purchase it so that I can give it to my niece for her birthday."

For days I sat paralyzed, waiting for him to ask me in person for the author's name, where I had purchased it, and so on. I had my "I lost it" ready, knowing that my answer would probably make me suspect. He never did ask me.

To this day, I don't know if he ever suspected anything. One thing was for sure: that terrible feeling that I carried with me for the weeks after the incident prevented me from ever pulling that kind of a stunt again!

Cheating and Its Consequences

I cheated on an exam once in second grade. I had studied diligently for a history test. One question asked for a list of three things that led to some specific incident. Having rehearsed that list repeatedly the night before, I confidently wrote down two, and then my mind went blank. Try as I might, I couldn't remember the others. Closing my eyes, I could picture the page of my outline, see the exact position of the three causes, but I could not read them. Time grew short.

"It's not fair," I thought. "I studied hard, I know the answer, I just can't think." It wasn't my fault, I reasoned. So I opened my desk, took out my notebook, and flipped to the page. A single glance and the answer came flooding back. My heart raced and the blood rushing to my head pounded so loudly in my ears, I was sure everyone in the room could hear it. No one noticed. I wiped my sweaty palms on my dress. My hand shook as I wrote the right answer and my stomach churned. I imagined myself standing in front of Mrs. O'Brien.

"You cheated. Why? You always got good marks. You don't need to cheat."

"But I wasn't really cheating," I wailed. "I knew the answer. I studied it last night. I just couldn't remember."

"But you did cheat and you will have to be punished." I could see her hand trace a big red F across the top of my paper.

"I will speak to your parents," she promised sternly. "I'm sure they will be as disappointed in you as I am."

My parents. What would they do? They'd be so ashamed of me. And my classmates. I could hear their jeer. My whole body was shaking now. Why had I ever taken such a chance?

I didn't get caught. I got away with cheating, but I was never tempted to cheat again—ever.

Becoming Aware of Thinking

I was in first grade when this happened. We had a girl in our class named Barbara who used to get out of her seat all the time and this irritated Mrs. Wyman, my teacher. So Mrs. Wyman tied Barbara into her chair and Barbara wet her pants. I was so embarrassed for her and felt so badly for her. Then I remembered that I was talking to myself in my head and I thought, "Do all the other boys and girls talk to themselves in their head?" I think that was the first time I was aware of thinking, the thought process. And it was the first time I was aware of thinking about thinking.

A Nice Sensation

Here is something that I remember that I found to be very satisfying. It has to do with learning something. And what it was is that I have kind of a recollection, perhaps more of a sensation, because I can't pin it down particularly. I suppose I was probably in the eighth grade or ninth grade in junior high school. Wherever it was that kids were taught how to do square root. I can remember the feeling of satisfaction I got at having learned to do just that. I sure couldn't do it today but I do remember feeling good that I had mastered square root. I'm not sure about this, but maybe the reason is that there is a certain symmetry to doing a square root. That is, you do it and then you know you've done it right because you multiply the answer by itself and you have the original number. So, that's the one thing I can remember. It's not the actual mechanics but I can remember the sensation of having done it and done it correctly.

How Much I Really Did Want to Learn

I think one of the turning points in learning for me was the time that I really wasn't doing very well all the way around in high school. I was taking a course in physiology and it was the kind of thing that was fairly advanced. We had to do what was called a physiology notebook by the end of the year. It was a 365-some-odd-page notebook. I did it on my own. It's interesting that at the time I felt like I was kind of on the line. My whole perception of learning, I think, really changed in such a way that I really clarified probably rather quickly how much learning really did mean to me and how much I really did want to learn.

This guy who was teaching it had the name of MacDeever. He was an interesting sort of character and I'm sure a lot of it had to do with his presentation. I felt comfortable there. So probably all the groundwork was laid. I think it really is a good example of just the learning process itself. I think that what I became aware of is that learning itself meant something to me. I think that what happened is that it was a point of question as to whether I was going to be able to do it. It was the doing of it. The reading of it and then the preparing of it. There were certain graphics to it. I still have it today. I look back and think that as a junior it was really a tough situation in my life. It really kind of shows that obviously I was into it. It was kind of neat.

I Learned to Calm Myself Down

In sixth grade, I was chosen to write a play that was then selected by the local state college for production. I starred in it when it was produced at the college. I remember standing under the Christmas tree. It was Christmastime and Miss Milton, our principal, came over to me and congratulated me, first of all for representing our school at the college and secondly for being in the play. But she said to me, "Ginny, I must tell you, the play was wonderful but you have a very piercing voice and you must learn to modulate your voice when you speak before an audience." To this day when I'm on the telephone or speaking into a speaker, my voice changes because I think of Miss Milton. If I stand in front of my classroom and I get carried away, because I do, I think of Miss Milton and calm myself down and speak in the lower level. And I'm 51 years old.

A Conceptual Linkage

This is a story about writing a term paper. I think it was in the seventh grade in a science class. We had to write a term paper and it was the first one I had ever written, I think, or one of the first ones. I was really interested at the time in schizophrenia. That was my big thing. And I was into art, too. And somehow or another I had some books on art drawn and painted by mental patients, so I was really into that and I was really reading about it. My father also got Harper's magazine, and at the time there had been an article about the modern scientific discovery of hallucinogenic mushrooms and LSD. I even think there was an article written by whoever it was who was able to invent LSD.

Anyway, at the time I certainly didn't know anything about drugs or their common street usage. But I was really interested in this article about hallucinogenics. It seemed to me that there was definitely something about what I remembered seeing in the pictures drawn and painted by the schizophrenics that related to the article that described what LSD did to people's minds.

So I remember writing the paper called "LSD and Schizophrenia, a Conceptual Linkage" in a completely naive fashion. And I remember that my science teacher was quite surprised at the topic and yet asked me if I would read my report to the class, which I did. I don't have any recollection of anybody else who knew what it meant, but I was definitely verging on something of great import. I didn't know that in a few short years people would be using hallucinogenics. It was something that I sort of discovered. I felt really good about it. Again, I remember talking about putting these ideas together at the dining room table and I remember my father talking about the conceptual linkage and I liked that a lot.

The Chess Tournament

A vivid moment that I remember was in the eighth grade. It was the chess tournament that they had, and for some reason I had gotten hooked into it although I wasn't an avid chess player. But I got very excited about it and I went out and bought a book or two on chess. I played and played for a week or two before this thing began, and what I remember very vividly is getting all the way to the finals. I remember one other person and I sitting after school in this classroom with nobody else in the school. He and I had no judges in the showdown. We had one of those little tables, one of those rickety desks. And we ended up playing 3 hours of chess. It was incredibly intense, very quiet. We were able to concentrate completely on what we were doing. He ended up winning. I learned, though, not only that I could do things well—because I hadn't been playing chess, and I had done very well in this—but that there were still people who could do better.

We Flew Kites to Learn About the Winds

We had a fourth-grade teacher who was very quiet and reserved. She was a good teacher and she was nice, but not terribly interesting. Halfway through the year, a student teacher came into our room and charged the air with his excitement and enthusiasm. He was a dynamic teacher and every activity he planned for us caught the interest of the whole class. I don't remember there being any kids getting in trouble either. I guess he didn't need to worry much about discipline. We flew kites to learn about the winds, we took nature walks to learn about our environment, we painted and put on plays to help us understand the different times and places we were learning about. We were never bored and almost never sat at our desks. It was the kind of experience easy to remember because of its uniqueness and interest and our fascination. He was a model for me when I became a teacher because he really taught us what it meant to learn through experience.

III

Conclusion: What All This Means for Educators

As we noted in chapter 1, our intent was to keep our own comments about the content of *The Unwritten Curriculum* to a minimum. It was more important, we thought, simply to let the memories of school that supplied the content for the curriculum tell the story with little elaboration on our part. In retrospect, it seems to have been a good decision. As we read and reread this collection of stories about school, it seemed to us that what our informants had to say about their memories, whether short or long, is much more important than an attempt on our part to interpret it.

Nevertheless, at the close of things, we want to raise and deal briefly with questions such as, What is to be made of all this? How should the information be viewed? What can be learned from it? Are there any implications for how school people, particularly teachers and principals, might want to change how they think about their work? Chapter 12 focuses on these questions.

Being Aware and Learning to Nurture

I t is our hope that this book broadens—with sometimes painful detail and sometimes heartwarming detail—the not-often-talked-about view of what school is like for kids. It is certainly not a view provided by school districts in individual brochures that talk about their curriculum and about what a youngster may be expected to learn. It would not be terribly politic on the part of a school to advertise to parents, for example, that their child is likely to have an embarrassing experience during his or her school years. Nevertheless, it is a pretty good bet that this will happen at some point in time during the school years—just as it is a pretty good bet that the child will experience being cared for by an adult and thus learn a bit more about what caring means.

All of this is not to deny that what schools are essentially and most appropriately about is the written curriculum: teaching youngsters to read, to write, to compute, to understand their own and other cultures, and so forth. No one would dispute that, but no single memory in our research involved the written curriculum in any detailed fashion or depth. This is quite understandable. After all, some of us can easily recall the excitement of reading our first story, but learning to read is hardly a single event that can be remembered.

116

As we think about the implications of the idea that this book represents part of the broader curriculum of the schools, we have in mind a point that we mentioned earlier. It is that the essential difference between the experiences these memories represent and those that might be associated with similar experience in one's family life is the social context in which they take place. It is likely, for example, that for most of the memory categories of school that are part of this book, each of us could think of one connected with our family life. We all can remember situations in which we felt unjustly treated by our parents (or so we thought at the time). We also know that, for most of us, even though we had this feeling, it eventually passed, and our family life resumed its balance through its natural nurturing patterns. In fact, it is the family's goal as a social system to do precisely that: return to its balance.

A school, though, is not a family unit and by definition is not a nurturing institution, although there are many nurturing *individuals* in them. For our purposes, this is a very important distinction to make. The essential reason for the family's existence as the basic social unit in just about every culture is its focus on the nurturance of its members. Such is not the case with the institution of the school, although many people would like to think it should be. Schools are focused on the work of learning. If a pupil happens to be nurtured or cared for during the whole process, nobody objects. But that is not the mission of the *school*. The reader may recall, for example, one woman's memory of embarrassment when, as a little girl, she was not permitted to go to the bathroom when she needed to, and she wet her pants. But also recall her memory of the teacher who comforted her. The need to comfort was the teacher's and not the school's. The point is that it is an imperative—sometimes honored in the breach, we suspect—that families hold their membership together through the glue of warmth, affection, and intimacy. There is no such imperative in the schools. Whatever the glue is that holds schools together, it includes nurturing only by chance and not by any systematic mandate. This is true even though, as we indicated above, many people would like it to be otherwise. Further, this is not to say that even if schools were systemically nurturant they would provide a better educative experience, although we certainly believe this would be the case. It is just to note that at this point in time it is not the guiding principle of school organizational life. However, we have little doubt that if schools were systematically nurturant, they would be more pleasant places for adults and youngsters alike.

Our point is, then, that going to school is indeed preparation for life in a world of work, but in ways that go much beyond the learning of basic skills, French, chemistry, history, and so on. Indeed, going to school and unavoidably engaging in the unwritten curriculum that the memories in this book describe is truly a valid start for a "learning about life" education.

These thoughts lead us to some comments about how the book may be used by people involved in, or soon to be involved in, the schools—student teachers, teachers, and administrators.

With regard to student teachers, it seems clear to us that consideration of the unwritten curriculum fills an important niche as prospective teachers engage in their student-teaching experience. It is not sufficient, we think, for student teachers to focus only on becoming a good classroom manager, or a good teacher of reading, social studies, or mathematics. Whatever the word "good" in those and other teaching fields means, we believe student teachers also need to understand the nature of the unwritten curriculum (which they, too, have experienced) and what parts of it their behavior "teaches" in the classroom.

Concerning in-service teachers and administrators, what is really at stake in any consideration of the unwritten curriculum is the character of the memories their current students will hold in 25 years relative to what school was about. What memory would Teacher X want his or her students to carry through a lifetime—bearing in mind for example, that no matter how good X is at teaching math, the students probably will not remember having learned to do long division? Similarly, what memory of their contact with Principal Y would he or she want students to carry with them throughout their lifetime? These are questions we think teachers and administrators as individuals should address, as well as the faculty as a group.

The importance of these questions, as we remarked in chapter 1, is underscored by the fact that in the great majority of memories that we have recounted in this book, the names and faces of the individuals involved were remembered—whether the memory was warm and comforting or harsh and punishing. Each of us as teacher or administrator would do well to keep this in mind.

Finally, we expect that most people who read this book will find that it exercises their own memory. It is fair to say that part of what a person may take from this book is the triggering of a recollection of school, usually with a smile, even though the remembered event may have felt very traumatic at the time. And there is an important thing to learn from that reaction. It is that, in the long run, isolated traumatic events tend, for the most part, to be remembered as part of the substance of what life itself is all about. Eventually, these events are treated with equanimity or even with humor, as we noted early on.

The reader may recall, for example, the short story of the third grader in chapter 1 whose teacher hit him with a ruler, without rhyme or reason as far as he could see. We know this person fairly well. When he told this story to us, he laughed. He is a very gentle person whose adult life, we feel quite sure, has not been emotionally hobbled by that event. We do not wish to make light of what happened, of course. It is sad to know it occurred in a school. But bullying, too, is a part of life, and most of us have been bullied at one time or another. We also have managed, however, to extricate ourselves from these situations—and have then tucked our memories of them away in what, again for most of us, is a hiding place for traumatic memories that become benign over time.

This last point lets us close the book with a broad invitation to the reader—whether you are a student, teacher, administrator, or school-oriented layperson—to use it as a vehicle for thinking about the schools of today in light of your own youthful experience. In this sense, we think that the book has the potential to serve as a prompting agent for each of us to think about, to talk about, and to better understand what it means to go to school.

References

Bruner, J. S. (1987). Life as narrative. *Social Research, 54*(1), 11-31.
Cowell, R. (1972). *The hidden curriculum.* Cambridge, MA: Harvard University, Graduate School of Education.
King, N. R. (1976). *The hidden curriculum and the socialization of kindergarten children.* Madison: University of Wisconsin-Madison.
Snyder, B. (1971). *The hidden curriculum.* New York: Knopf.
Stone, E. (1988, January 24). Stories make a family. *New York Times Magazine*, pp. 29-30.